SINGING WITH EXPRESSION

A Guide to Authentic & Adventurous Song Interpretation

By Rosana Eckert

PLAYBACK+
Speed • Pitch • Balance • Loop

HAL•LEONARD®

7777 W. BLUEMOUND RD. P.O. BOX 13819 MILWAUKEE, WI 53213

ISBN 978-1-4950-9543-6

In Australia Contact:
Hal Leonard Australia Pty. Ltd.
4 Lentara Court
Cheltenham, Victoria, 3192 Australia
Email: ausadmin@halleonard.com.au

Visit Hal Leonard Online at
www.halleonard.com

CONTENTS

SECTION 1
TIMING: PHRASE IT LIKE YOU SAY IT

CHAPTER 1. RUBATO PHRASING

CHAPTER 2. RUBATO/RHYTHMIC PHRASING COMBO

CHAPTER 3. RHYTHMIC PHRASING – MEDIUM AND UP-TEMPO

CHAPTER 4. EXPLORING OTHER GROOVES

SECTION 2
TONE: COLOR IT LIKE YOU SAY IT

CHAPTER 5. VOCAL TECHNIQUE BASICS

CHAPTER 6. FURTHER TONAL EXPLORATION

SECTION 3
MELODIC ALTERATIONS: SHAPE IT LIKE YOU SAY IT

CHAPTER 7. SMALL GESTURES

CHAPTER 8. LARGE GESTURES

SECTION 4
STYLE: EXPRESS IT LIKE YOU SAY IT

CHAPTER 9. EXPLORING STYLISTIC GESTURES

CHAPTER 10. EXPLORING STYLE THROUGH
DEEP TRANSCRIPTION AND IMITATION

SECTION 5
ADDITIONAL FACTORS

CHAPTER 11. THE VISUAL EFFECT

CHAPTER 12. CHOOSING REPERTOIRE

INTRODUCTION

One of my favorite musical memories is the night I heard Nancy King sing live at the Jazz Standard in New York City. She was captivating, adventurous, artistic, and genuine. I wept through half of her performance out of sheer joy and appreciation. Several years later, I had the pleasure of seeing her perform at a different venue, and once again, I was affected in a profound way. I love that type of artist. It is a special thing to hear a singer who can draw the listener in completely, creating a shared experience of stories and emotions – a singer who can surprise us, inspire us, make us laugh, make us cry, make us feel included – a singer who has a clear point of view and is able to communicate it genuinely.

In my own journey as a singer and voice teacher, I have made it my life's work to try and hone in on the diverse elements that give singers both a unique voice and a connection with their audiences. This book is a collection of concepts and exercises developed over many years of listening, singing, and teaching. It is meant to serve singers of various styles of music.

HOW TO USE THIS BOOK

Singing with Expression is separated into five sections: Timing, Tone, Melodic Alteration, Style, and Other Factors. Throughout the book, you'll find a step-by-step approach to each concept, and within each chapter, the exercises are meant to be worked in order. Downloadable listening tracks are included with this book and contain my vocal demonstrations as well as backing tracks for you to use in your practice.

The backing tracks are available in three keys. My demonstrations are done in keys suitable for alto voices. If you would like to use the alto key as your backing track without my vocal guide, locate the tracks that say "alto key," and simply pan the balance to the left side to eliminate the vocal demonstration. There are also backing tracks in keys suitable for most soprano voices and tenor/baritone voices. Additionally, these recordings utilize the *PLAYBACK+* feature, making it possible to independently adjust the key, tempo, and balance.

In the back of the book, you will find a listening list of recordings that specifically demonstrate a groove or approach discussed in the book. Listening is a key part of the process!

Some chapters include spontaneity exercises, meant to help you sharpen your reflexes so that you can react quickly to ever-changing performance situations. Think of how many different variables there are from gig to gig: your performance venue, audience members, band members, performance attire, vocal health, overall frame of mind and mood, time of year, etc. The list is long, and each element can potentially affect the way you feel like approaching a song. This book offers numerous ways to build a "mental library" of interpretation concepts that will allow you to follow your instincts and stay present when you perform. If you let the music truly reflect how you feel in the moment, you will never sing a song the same way twice. Rather, you will create a unique and authentic experience for your audience, your band, and yourself – every time.

–Rosana Eckert

IT'S YOU

Music and Lyrics by
Rosana Eckert

IT'S YOU

When I open up my eyes to greet the morning,
And the dancing dreams that filled the night are through,
I can hear the sweetest melody, a whisper in my ear.
It's you, it's you.

When I'm strolling to the café on the corner,
And the sun is smiling on the ocean blue,
I am cradled by the memory of yesterday's embrace.
It's you, it's you.

I remember how we used to walk the shore,
Seeing summers we had never seen before.
I remember how we thought that it would last forevermore,
But the autumn came with a sudden rain.

When I'm sitting by the window in the moonlight,
And I wonder how I'll ever make it through,
There's a spirit in my heart that wants to sing tomorrow's song.
It's you, it's you.

DANCE WITH ME

Music and Lyrics by
Rosana Eckert

DANCE WITH ME

Dance with me. There's magic in the night.
Dream with me beneath the starry light.
I sent my wish to the sky.
My heart is ready to fly.

Oh, won't you sway with me, a tango just for two?
Could it be I'll fall in love with you?
And we would be such a sight.
Just dance with me tonight.

SECTION 1
Timing:
Phrase It Like You Say It

They say the secret to great comedy is… timing. Well, the same is true for delivering a great song lyric. In fact, let's consider timing (as in, the length of time spent on syllables and spaces) as the "protein" on our song interpretation plate. We'll add wonderful "veggies" and "grains" in other sections, but the protein is what will really fill your listener up.

CHAPTER 1
Rubato Phrasing

Rubato phrasing is phrasing that is not rhythmically connected to a particular subdivision or groove. Rather, the lyrics are sung freely, inspired by natural speech. The singer is free to push and pull the pacing of the words.

EXERCISE 1
RESEARCHING THE LYRIC – "IT'S YOU"

"Researching" the lyric is the most important step. We'll use the song "It's You" for these exercises, but you can follow these procedures with every song you sing. Learn the song straight first, exactly as written on the sheet music. Then begin working from the lyric sheet.

 "It's You" – sung straight, ballad (alto key)
TRACK 1

Step 1: Understanding the Message
Recite the lyric of your song aloud. Ask yourself:

      What is the overall message of the story? Who is the speaker? Who is the recipient?

For "It's You":
- Message: Everywhere I go, I sense that you are there.
- Speaker: The singer, a person reminiscing.
- Recipient: Someone the singer cares for deeply, someone who is gone.

Step 2: Identifying Goal Words
Each phrase we speak or sing has a goal word, the highest point of emphasis or the most meaningful word in the phrase. When speaking, goal words typically have the highest vocal pitch or the most emphasis from the voice. Identify the goal word of each line by reciting them aloud; this will give you a better idea of how to shape and pace the lines once you start to sing. You can establish and communicate a point of view by shaping phrases around goal words, connecting more deeply with the listener.

    Decide on a goal word for each phrase of "It's You." Underline the word lightly in pencil on your lyric sheet. Read the lines aloud again. Emphasize the goal words by saying them more slowly and by pitching your speaking voice higher on those words.

    Note: The words around your goal word should be spoken more quickly.

Example:
    When I open up my EYES to greet the morning,
    And the dancing dreams that filled the NIGHT are through,
    I can hear the sweetest MELODY,
    A whisper in my EAR.
    It's YOU, it's you.

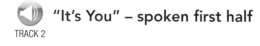 "It's You" – spoken first half
TRACK 2

Step 3: Changing It Up

Speak through the lyric again, this time using different important or expressive words as goal words. Sometimes we tend to gravitate toward goal words that are naturally emphasized by the melody. Exploring other goal options as we speak through the lyric helps us explore various interpretations of each line.

Example:

When I open up my eyes to GREET the morning,
And the dancing dreams that FILLED the night are through,
I can hear the SWEETEST melody,
A WHISPER in my ear.
It's you, it's YOU.

Go through each line of text in this way.

"It's You" – alternating goal words
TRACK 3

Step 4: Secondary Goal Words

Oftentimes, particularly with ballads, the phrases are long enough and wordy enough to have more than one goal word. "It's You" is an example of this type of song. Identify two goal words in each long phrase, a primary and a secondary. Speak through various options. Hold each goal word longer than the other words, with slightly more length to the primary goal word. Remember, all other words should be paced more quickly. If a goal word has two syllables, use a natural syllabic emphasis. Here are some examples of goal word combinations.

<u>PRIMARY GOAL WORD</u>   SECONDARY GOAL WORD

Examples:

When I open up my <u>EYES</u> to GREET the morning
When I open up my <u>EYES</u> to greet the MORNING
When I <u>OPEN</u> up my eyes to greet the MORNING

And the dancing DREAMS that filled the night are <u>THROUGH</u>
And the DANCING dreams that <u>FILLED</u> the night are through
And the dancing <u>DREAMS</u> that filled the NIGHT are through

Let's look at some lyrics from the bridge of the song:

I REMEMBER how we used to walk the <u>SHORE</u>
I remember how we <u>USED</u> to walk the SHORE
I REMEMBER how we used to <u>WALK</u> the shore

Seeing SUMMERS we had never <u>SEEN</u> before
Seeing summers we had <u>NEVER</u> seen BEFORE
Seeing <u>SUMMERS</u> we had never SEEN before

"It's You – primary and secondary goal words
TRACK 4

Note: If you feel a little self-conscious or embarrassed reading your lyric aloud with emotion, that's perfectly normal. This is why we do these exercises in the practice room and not at dinner parties. However, these are important steps, so just jump in and go for it!

Step 5: Adding the Melody

It's time to sing! Freely, sing each line of "It's You" *a cappella*. Don't try to keep a beat of any kind. Aim for the goal words you identified when you recited the lyric. Start with the most natural goal words, then change it up. Aim to sing the lines with the same speed of delivery (or a little slower) you used when speaking. Your pacing should differ greatly from the original rhythms on the sheet music. This phrasing will be your interpretation, your point of view. Remember to move more quickly through unimportant words so the goal words receive greater emphasis.

 "It's You" – first half sung *a cappella*, rubato
TRACK 5

EXERCISE 2
TAKING THE INTERPRETATION DEEPER

Step 1: Using Dramatic Pauses

When used thoughtfully, pauses can make a good lyric interpretation especially effective. Recite the lyric again, more slowly, using an even more dramatic approach, like you are acting on a stage in a huge theater. Take notice of where you insert pauses (large and small), which syllables get held the longest, and how you flow more quickly through unimportant words like "the" or "and." Mark these places on the lyric sheet. Take your time with this. Try each line a few times to find what feels natural. Record yourself if you find it hard to remember what you did. After you have experimented with a few different pause plans, try singing with those ideas. I find that I use dramatic pauses before or after (or both) a goal word. Here are two examples of possible large and small pauses in the first two lines.

> When I OPEN up my <u>EYES</u>^^ to greet the morning
> When I open up my <u>EYES</u>^^ to GREET^the morning

> And the dancing dreams that FILLED the <u>NIGHT</u>^^ are through
> And the dancing <u>DREAMS</u>^ that filled the night are THROUGH

 "It's You" – dramatic pauses, spoken and sung
TRACK 6

Step 2: Varying Phrase Lengths

Vocalists often want to sustain at the end of every phrase, but that can get predictable and seem less personal. Sing the song again, this time varying the length of the last syllable in each phrase. Try cutting a few of them shorter. How does this affect the mood or meaning?

 "It's You" – varying phrase endings
TRACK 7

EXERCISE 3
RUBATO PHRASING IN A DUO SETTING

When a singer and an instrumentalist perform a song together in a rubato style, the instrumentalist pushes and pulls the time with the singer. Though vocalists typically sing in a rubato style with only one other musician, it can be done with two or more players if everyone is on the same page with regard to phrasing.

Because the singer is delivering the lyric, it is usually their role to lead the phrasing in a rubato style. However, it is useful to think of the song as a conversation between two people, with the singer telling the story, and the other musician (a pianist, in this case) reacting and responding.

Step 1: Obvious Pushing and Pulling

Pushing and pulling the speed of phrases can keep rubato delivery from getting too slow or too predictable. In this exercise, we will experiment with the pushing and pulling two ways.

First, sing through "It's You" with rubato phrasing. Sing the first line with a quick overall pace, the second line with a slow overall pace, the third line with a quick pace, and so on. When delivering words quickly, continue to be expressive, but avoid long dramatic pauses or long sustains. Those lines will seem more casual and speech-like. When delivering words more slowly, use longer dramatic pauses and more sustains with your goal words.

Quickly   (quick release)   (quick release)
When I open up my EYES^ to greet the MORNING,

Slower, more dramatic (more sustained goal words) (sustain)
And the dancing dreams that FILLED the NIGHT^are through,

Slower   (sustain)
I can HEAR the sweetest MELODY,

Quickly   (quick release)
a WHISPER in my EAR.

Slowly Quickly
It's YOU, it's you.

Next, alternate slow pacing and quick pacing within a single phrase. In other words, sing the first part of the phrase at one speed and sing the second part of the phrase at another.

Slowly   Quickly
When I'm STROLLING to the CAFÉ on the corner,

Slowly   Quickly
And the sun is SMILING^ on the ocean BLUE,

Quickly   Slowly
I am cradled by the MEMORY ^of YESTERDAY'S embrace,

Quickly, Slowly
It's you, it's YOU.

Listen to Track 8 for an example of both of these pushing and pulling exercises.

🔊 **"It's You" – rubato pushing and pulling, *a cappella***
TRACK 8

Now listen to Track 9 to hear me use this push-and-pull plan in a duo setting with a pianist. Notice how the pianist responds to the vocal, as though in a conversation.

🔊 **"It's You" – rubato pushing and pulling with pianist**
TRACK 9

This is just one of many ways to treat this lyric. Changing the goal words, the pauses, and the approaches to the push-and-pull plan will lead to many different interpretations. The possibilities are endless and every version can be unique.

Step 2: Keeping the Ears Open

Using the push-and-pull plan from the previous exercise, sing along with Tracks 10 and 11, the rubato piano track for "It's You" with no vocal guide. While it is a little unnatural to practice duo rubato phrasing without being in the presence of another live player, you will get an idea of what it feels like to be in that musical conversation. Listening is key!

🔊 **"It's You" – rubato with pianist, backing track (soprano key)**
TRACK 10

🔊 **"It's You" – rubato with pianist, backing track (tenor/baritone key)**
TRACK 11

> **Tip:** In a live setting, listen for whether or not your musical partner is responding to your push-and-pull rubato phrasing. If you aren't "conversing" well, don't just plow ahead without him/her. You may have to do a bit more "following" until you have time to rehearse. A little friendly eye contact and even some small, gentle motions on each goal word can do the trick.

Rehearsing Rubato

If you are singing a song with an experienced pianist or guitarist who knows the song and is used to "conversing" with singers in a rubato style, you will likely need no rehearsal. However, if you find you are not on the same page, stepping on each other's toes, or unable to achieve the right phrasing for the lyric, some practice together would be beneficial. You will not necessarily be drilling the exact phrasing that will happen. (You could, but then there would be no spontaneity.) Rather, you will be preparing for the art of musical discourse. Track 12 demonstrates how piano fills can mirror actual conversation.

🔊 **"It's You" – rubato, piano responses as conversation**
TRACK 12

EXERCISE 4
RUBATO PHRASING IN A STRAIGHT BALLAD STYLE

In a *straight ballad style*, the instrumentalists keep a slow, steady tempo with a straight-eighth-note feel. When singing a straight ballad, we want to put the lyric across conversationally, using the same type of delivery as in the rubato push-and-pull-style. However, now we must keep track of beats and measures as the band is playing with a steady tempo.

Important: To maintain the same conversational pacing in this style, we need to incorporate *back-phrasing*. We do this by putting space at the beginning of the phrase, starting the lyric later than notated on the sheet music. This allows us to compress the lyrics, delivering them conversationally with rubato phrasing, at the back end of the phrase. Without back-phrasing, it is difficult to achieve a natural, conversational approach in a straight ballad style. Listen to the demonstration on Track 13 for an example.

🔊 **"It's You" – back-phrasing**
TRACK 13

Here is a written example of back-phrasing. The straight version of the melody is written on top, and the back-phrasing version is on the bottom.

Step 1: Singing with Back-phrasing

Using Tracks 14 and 15, sing each line using the back-phrasing technique. If this is new for you, wait one second before starting to sing each line. Instead of singing the pick-ups to each line before the downbeat, try singing them once the downbeat has passed.

 **"It's You"** – straight ballad, backing track (soprano key)
TRACK 14

 **"It's You"** – straight ballad, backing track (tenor/baritone key)
TRACK 15

Step 2: Exaggerating the Holds and Pauses

Sing along with the backing track again, this time holding the goal words even longer, and making the pauses even more dramatic within the lines. You should find that you "take up more space" in the measures this way, and the tempo doesn't feel as slow. Doing this could cause you to finish the phrase quite a bit later than notated on the sheet music. This is a problem only if back-phrasing causes the melody to clash with chords at any time. Practicing with a backing track is the key to knowing the back-phrasing options you have within the confines of the chord structure.

> **Tip:** Don't back-phrase each line in the exact same way. If you start each phrase three beats late without variation or "catching up," the band might start to think you are actually three beats off. Also, if you get too adventurous with back-phrasing, you might begin to create tension for the listener as they start to wonder if something is "off." Ideally you want back-phrasing to enhance, not distract.

EXERCISE 5
SPONTANEITY PRACTICE

Read a short excerpt from a newspaper, book, or magazine. Read slowly, deliberately, and expressively. Then, sing what you spoke, making up your own melody – no tempo, no groove. Use rubato phrasing. Spend more time on meaningful words. (Remember: Rubato doesn't mean slow; it means free to push and pull the time.)

 **spontaneity practice** – rubato phrasing
TRACK 16

CHAPTER 2
Rubato/Rhythmic Phrasing Combo

Explanation: *Rubato/rhythmic phrasing combo* incorporates both *rubato phrasing* and *rhythmic phrasing*.

Rubato phrasing: phrasing that avoids strict rhythm, with no connection to tempo or groove.

Rhythmic phrasing: phrasing that completely locks in with the tempo, groove, and subdivision at all times (also referred to as being "in-the-pocket").

This combo style of phrasing is good for slow, groove-based styles such as:
- Slow Swing
- Medium-Slow Swing
- Slow Bossa Nova
- Bolero (or slow Rhumba)
- Slow 12/8 (pop groove)

The slow tempo of these styles invites a free, rubato phrasing style. However, if there is an underlying groove, it is important to acknowledge it from time to time, to avoid sounding like you are unaware of what the band is doing.

To combine rubato phrasing with rhythmic phrasing successfully, we must practice rhythmic phrasing by itself.

EXERCISE 1
RHYTHMIC PHRASING – SLOW SWING

Listen to the example of rhythmic phrasing in "It's You," sung in a slow swing style with no goal word interpretation (Track 17). Notice how, in swing, the underlying subdivision is a triplet feel, giving the eighth notes a different placement than in a straight ballad.

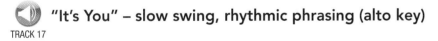 "It's You" – slow swing, rhythmic phrasing (alto key)
TRACK 17

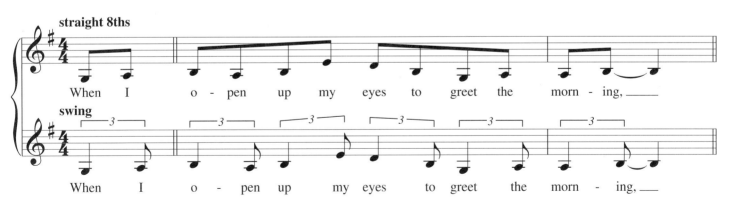

Sing "It's You" to one of the backing tracks (18/19), staying entirely in-the-pocket, without exception! In other words, keep all rhythms swinging, locking in with the triplet feel in every phrase. At this point, do not try to interpret the lyric. Focus on being *in-the-pocket* 100 percent of the time.

🔊 "It's You" – slow swing, backing track (soprano key)
TRACK 18

🔊 "It's You" – slow swing, backing track (tenor/baritone key)
TRACK 19

EXERCISE 2
APPLYING INTERPRETATION TO RHYTHMIC PHRASING – SLOW SWING

We will now apply lyric interpretation to "It's You" while staying *in-the-pocket* in a slow swing. Using the goal words below – or your own plan – practice swinging with interpretation. Stay in-the-pocket at all times at this point. We can acknowledge the goal words as we did in a ballad, holding them a little longer, inserting small and large pauses, and varying the length of the last note. We simply need to remain aware of the triplet feel, now that we are in a swing style. You might find it difficult to stay rhythmically in the pocket on every phrase. Practice until you can do this. Repetition is important, like batting practice for a baseball player.

Practice swinging *with interpretation* in these three ways:
- Speak the swing rhythms *a cappella*; use a metronome set at 64 beats per minutes (bpm).
- Speak the swing rhythms to the backing track (18/19).
- Sing with the backing track (18/19).

You can listen to a demonstration of these three "with interpretation" practice techniques on the following tracks:

🔊 "It's You" – spoken swinging, with metronome
TRACK 20

🔊 "It's You" – spoken swinging, with backing track
TRACK 21

🔊 "It's You" – sung swinging, with backing track
TRACK 22

I used this goal word plan for my demonstration. Primary goal words are underlined:

When I OPEN up my EYES to greet the morning,
And the DANCING dreams that filled the NIGHT are through,
I can HEAR the sweetest MELODY, a WHISPER in my ear.
It's YOU, it's you.

When I'm STROLLING to the café on the CORNER,
And the SUN is SMILING on the ocean blue,
I am CRADLED by the memory of yesterday's EMBRACE.
It's you, it's YOU

I REMEMBER how we used to WALK the shore,
Seeing SUMMERS we had never SEEN before.
I remember HOW we thought that it would LAST forevermore,
But the AUTUMN came with a sudden RAIN.

When I'm SITTING by the WINDOW in the moonlight,
And I wonder HOW I'll EVER make it through,
There's a SPIRIT in my heart that wants to SING tomorrow's song.
It's you, it's YOU.

Here is an example of how the goal-word plan for the first eight bars could be delivered with rhythmic phrasing.

Keep in mind, when you spend more time on a goal word, you may get a little behind in the timing for the rest of the phrase. Don't worry! Practice with the backing track to see if ending the phrase later conflicts with the chords. Your ear will let you know. If you run into a problem with chords clashing, try starting the phrase earlier (not back-phrasing as much), or going more quickly after the goal word. It takes practice to find all the available rhythmic options you could employ to make your goal words stand out.

EXERCISE 3
ALTERNATING RUBATO AND RHYTHMIC PHRASING – SLOW SWING

Now that we are familiar with both rubato phrasing (Chapter 1) and rhythmic phrasing, let's combine these two concepts.

Step 1: Alternating Phrase by Phrase

Begin by singing the first phrase with rubato phrasing. Then sing the second phrase with rhythmic phrasing. In this case, the phrases will alternate phrasing style two measures at a time. Continue this pattern, phrase by phrase, in this way. When you get to a new section of a song, reverse the phrasing order, as notated below. Listen to the recorded example of this alternating phrasing plan using the goal shown here.

Rubato Phrasing:	When I open up my <u>EYES</u> to greet the <u>MORNING</u>,
Rhythmic Phrasing:	And the <u>DANCING</u> dreams that <u>FILLED</u> the night are through,
Rubato Phrasing:	I can <u>HEAR</u> the sweetest <u>MELODY</u>, a <u>WHISPER</u> in my ear.
Rhythmic Phrasing:	It's <u>YOU</u>, it's you.

Rhythmic Phrasing:	When I'm <u>STROLLING</u> to the café on the <u>CORNER</u>,
Rubato Phrasing:	And the sun is <u>SMILING</u> on the ocean <u>BLUE</u>,
Rhythmic Phrasing:	I am <u>CRADLED</u> by the memory of yesterday's <u>EMBRACE</u>.
Rubato Phrasing:	It's you, it's <u>YOU</u>.

🔊 **"It's You" – slow swing, alternating rubato and rhythmic phrasing (two bars)**
TRACK 23

Step 2: Exploring Other Phrasing Patterns

Explore other ways to alternate between these two phrasing styles. For example, you could try changing phrasing styles every measure instead of every two measures. That might look like this:

Rhythmic: When I open up my EYES	Rubato: to greet the MORNING,
Rhythmic: And the dancing DREAMS	Rubato: that FILLED the night are through,
Rhythmic: I can HEAR the sweetest melody,	Rubato: a WHISPER in my ear.
Rhythmic: It's YOU,	Rubato: IT'S you.

🔊 **"It's You" – slow swing, alternating rubato and rhythmic phrasing (one bar)**
TRACK 24

You could also experiment with other phrasing combinations (2:1, 1:2, etc.), using slow groove-based styles. As noted earlier, the rubato phrasing suits the slow tempo, and the rhythmic phrasing suits the underlying groove. This is why using a combination of both is appropriate. Using only rubato phrasing in a slow groove style can make the vocals sound unaware of the groove. This might create tension for the listener and a feeling of disconnect with the band. On the other hand, using only rhythmic phrasing at this slow tempo can get a bit monotonous or predictable. It's nice to play against the groove sometimes and build phrasing tension in that way. The return to rhythmic phrasing after a couple of rubato phrases can have a remarkable releasing effect.

EXERCISE 4
RHYTHMIC PHRASING – STRAIGHT-EIGHTH BOSSA NOVA

Let's switch grooves and sing in a Brazilian bossa nova style! Bossa nova rose to popularity in the United States in the early 1960s with the release of the legendary recording *Gilberto/Getz*, a collaboration between Brazilian vocalist/guitarist Joao Gilberto and American jazz saxophonist Stan Getz. Their style fused Brazilian samba with jazz and highlighted a more "chill" way to play and sing Brazilian samba. If bossa nova is a new groove for you, take time to listen to traditional bossa nova. Start with the Brazilian classics "The Girl from Ipanema" and "Corcovado" by Antonio Carlos Jobim. There are other Brazilian artists and songs recommended on the listening page at the back of this book.

We will continue to use "It's You." To make this song feel natural in a bossa nova style, we will incorporate a double-time feel. Our tempo will decrease slightly to 50 bpm. Using a double-time feel means the band will read the music at 50 bpm, but will play the groove such that it "feels" like they are playing at 100 bpm. This technique often works well when you are transferring ballads to bossa nova, but you still want the singing to have a slow ballad delivery. (We'll look at double-time feel in more depth in Chapter 4.)

Step 1: Exploring Off-Beats

Many traditional bossa nova melodies include a lot of off-beat rhythms (consecutive syncopation). Thus, it can sound very natural to do this when interpreting a song in the bossa nova style. Sing through "It's You" in its entirety, using only off-beats, disregarding goal words. The rhythmic change looks like this:

Step 2: Rhythmic Phrasing

Listen to Track 25, "It's You" sung completely in-the-pocket with a bossa nova groove, utilizing some of the off-beat rhythms noted above. Then try it yourself using a backing track (26/27). Remember, at this point, we are not trying to interpret the lyric. We are merely trying to stay in-the-pocket all the time.

"It's You" – bossa nova, rhythmic phrasing (alto key)

TRACK 25

"It's You" – bossa nova, backing track (soprano key)

TRACK 26

"It's You" – bossa nova, backing track (tenor/baritone key)

TRACK 27

EXERCISE 5
APPLYING INTERPETATION TO RHYTHMIC PHRASING – BOSSA NOVA

Now let's apply lyric interpretation to "It's You" while using exclusively rhythmic phrasing. We can use the same approach with straight-eighth grooves as with swing. By emphasizing goal words dynamically or holding them longer, we can add meaningful expression. Strive to do this while staying in-the-pocket. Remember that syncopation is a natural phrasing tool for grooves like bossa nova. As with Exercise 2 in this chapter, it is important to get to the place where you can interpret the lyric while staying in-the-pocket 100 percent of the time.

Practice bossa nova with interpretation in these three ways:
- Speak the straight-eighth rhythms *a cappella*, using a metronome set to 100 bpm (Track 28).
- Speak the straight-eighth rhythms to the backing track (Track 29).
- Sing with the backing track (Track 30).

You can listen to a demonstration of these three "with interpretation" practice techniques on the following tracks:

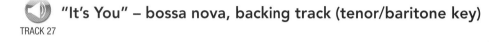

"It's You" – bossa nova, spoken, interpretation with metronome

TRACK 28

"It's You" – bossa nova, spoken, interpretation with backing track

TRACK 29

"It's You" – bossa nova, sung, interpretation with backing track

TRACK 30

Here is a demonstration of the entire chorus of "It's You," written out with interpreted rhythmic phrasing. The goal word plan is shown on page 17. (Primary goal words are underlined.)

When I open up my <u>EYES</u> to greet the MORNING,
And the DANCING dreams that filled the <u>NIGHT</u> are through,
I can HEAR the sweetest <u>MELODY</u>, a WHISPER in my ear.
It's YOU, it's you.

When I'm <u>STROLLING</u> to the café on the CORNER,
And the SUN is <u>SMILING</u> on the ocean blue,
I am <u>CRADLED</u> by the memory of yesterday's EMBRACE.
It's you, it's YOU.

I REMEMBER how we used to <u>WALK</u> the shore,
Seeing SUMMERS we had never <u>SEEN</u> before.
I remember HOW we thought that it would <u>LAST</u> forevermore,
But the <u>AUTUMN</u> came with a sudden RAIN.

When I'm SITTING by the <u>WINDOW</u> in the moonlight,
And I wonder HOW I'll <u>EVER</u> make it through,
There's a <u>SPIRIT</u> in my heart that wants to SING tomorrow's song.
It's you, it's YOU.

EXERCISE 6
ALTERNATING RUBATO AND RHYTHMIC PHRASING – BOSSA NOVA

Let's try the phrasing combo with bossa nova. We'll use the same process of an organized "off and on" as we did with swing in Exercise 3.

Step 1: Alternating Phrase by Phrase
Using the backing track for bossa nova (26/27), sing "It's You," alternating rubato and rhythmic phrasing every two measures.

Step 2: Exploring Other Phrasing Patterns
Think of other ways to alternate between rubato and rhythmic phrasing (2:1, 1:2). For a more detailed explanation of this process, refer back to Exercise 3 in this chapter.

Listen to the recorded examples of these exercises.

🔊 **"It's You" – bossa nova, alternating rubato and rhythmic phrasing (two bars)**
TRACK 31

🔊 **"It's You" – bossa nova, alternating rubato and rhythmic phrasing (one bar)**
TRACK 32

EXERCISE 7
SPONTANEITY PRACTICE

Take a poem, short story, or different song lyric and speak the words rhythmically with a metronome set to 80-90 bpm. Have a groove in your mind (swing, straight-eighth, etc.). First work to use rhythmic phrasing exclusively, then do the alternating exercise. This is a spontaneity exercise because you must come up with your rhythmic ideas and goal words in real time, without having worked them out step-by-step.

🔊 **spontaneity practice, rhythmic phrasing**
TRACK 33

CHAPTER 3
Rhythmic Phrasing – Medium and Up-tempo

Rhythmic phrasing is phrasing that is rhythmically locked into the groove at all times. We introduced rhythmic phrasing in Chapter 2 when we explored alternating between rubato and rhythmic phrasing. Refer to that chapter for rhythmic phrasing exercises at a slower tempo.

In this chapter, we will focus on medium and fast grooves. When singing at a quicker tempo, it is best to stay *in-the-pocket* all or most of the time. The quicker the tempo, the higher the ratio of rhythmic phrasing. At 250 bpm, you should be in-the-pocket completely. You can be as adventurous with your phrasing as you want as long as you are locking in with the time-feel, connecting with the rhythmic subdivision. Remember: When you sing these styles of music, you are *part of* the band, as opposed to being *accompanied by* the band. All parties are responsible for the groove and time-feel, even the singer. If everyone locks in with the rhythm, the music will feel and sound great.

Rhythmic phrasing works well with medium-to-fast grooves, including:
- Medium-to-fast swing
- Brazilian styles (samba, medium-to-fast bossa nova)
- Medium-to-fast ballroom Latin or Afro-Cuban Grooves (cha-cha, rhumba, mambo, etc.)
- Pop grooves

New Song: "Dance with Me"
Let's change songs for this next set of exercises. While "It's You" can be sung quickly and with different grooves, it has a lot of lyrics, which limits our rhythmic options at a fast tempo. We'll use "Dance with Me" for the exercises in this chapter.

EXERCISE 1
RESEARCHING THE LYRIC – "DANCE WITH ME"

Before digging into the various steps in this exercise, use the lead sheet for "Dance with Me" (page xi) and the audio track (34) to learn the song *straight*. Once you have memorized the melody, switch to using the lyric sheet and begin the steps.

🔊 **"Dance with Me" – medium swing, sung straight (alto key)**
TRACK 34

Step 1: Understanding the Message
Recite the lyric aloud and get the big picture, as we did in Chapter 1. Consider the following: What is the overall message of the story? Who is the speaker? Who is the recipient?

> Dance with me. There's magic in the night.
> Dream with me beneath the starry light.
> I sent my wish to the sky.
> My heart is ready to fly.

Oh, won't you sway with me, a tango just for two?
Could it be I'll fall in love with you?
And we would be such a sight.
Just dance with me tonight.

Step 2: Identifying Goal Words

Identify primary and secondary goal words. (See Chapter 1 for more instruction.) Try a few different combinations of goal words. Circle your favorites with a pencil on your lyric sheet; use a pencil so you have the option to change goal words and vary the interpretation. Speak through these goal-word possibilities or try your own combination. As we did in Chapter 1, speak slowly and deliberately, like you are acting out these words. Let the tone of your speaking voice rise on the goal words, and experiment with sustaining them a bit longer, even when speaking.

 "Dance with Me" – lyric spoken two ways

TRACK 35

Version 1
<u>DANCE</u> with me. There's <u>MAGIC</u> in the night.
<u>DREAM</u> with me <u>BENEATH</u> the starry light.
I sent my <u>WISH</u> to the <u>SKY</u>.
My heart is <u>READY</u> to <u>FLY</u>.

Oh, won't you <u>SWAY</u> with me, a <u>TANGO</u> just for two?
Could it <u>BE</u> I'll <u>FALL</u> in love with you?
And we would be <u>SUCH</u> a <u>SIGHT</u>.
Just <u>DANCE</u> with me <u>TONIGHT</u>.

Version 2
Dance with <u>ME</u>. There's magic in the <u>NIGHT</u>.
<u>DREAM</u> with me beneath the <u>STARRY</u> light.
I sent my <u>WISH</u> to the <u>SKY</u>.
My <u>HEART</u> is ready to <u>FLY</u>.

Oh, won't you sway with <u>ME</u>, a tango <u>JUST</u> for two?
Could it <u>BE</u> I'll fall in <u>LOVE</u> with you?
And <u>WE</u> would be <u>SUCH</u> a sight.
Just <u>DANCE</u> with <u>ME</u> tonight.

Step 3: Adding the Melody

Finally, sing the tune with the medium-swing audio tracks (36/37), trying to interpret the lyric. You might attempt a few different goal-word plans. Note: With the increased tempo and rhythmic delivery, it may be difficult to distinguish between primary goal words and secondary goal words; you may find you decrease the number of goal words in a phrase as the tempo increases.

 "Dance with Me" – medium swing, backing track (soprano key)

TRACK 36

 "Dance with Me" – medium swing, backing track (tenor/baritone key)

TRACK 37

EXERCISE 2
RESTRICTIVE RHYTHM PRACTICE – MEDIUM SWING

Let's get acquainted with some of our rhythmic options at a medium tempo before moving on to faster speeds. Remember: When using rhythmic phrasing, make an effort to stay in-the-pocket 100 percent of the time. Don't attempt any interpretation in this exercise; simply explore the rhythmic phrasing options. Using the audio tracks for "Dance with Me" (36/37), sing all the way through the song three times, in each instance using one of the following rhythmic restrictions:

    1. **Syncopation:** Use as much syncopation as you can, with many consecutive off-beat rhythms for lines that have a lot of quarter notes.

    2. **Dotted-Quarter Note:** Repeat this dotted-quarter note pattern, starting over every four bars. The effect is a hemiola pattern, which sounds like 3/4 time over 4/4 time.

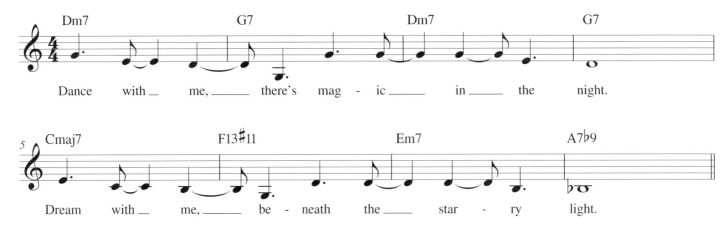

3. Eighth-Note Groupings: Incorporate back-phrasing as we did in straight ballad singing in Chapter 1, as a way to group eighth notes together.

Listen to Track 38 for examples of all three rhythmic restriction exercises.

🔊 **"Dance with Me" – medium swing, restrictive rhythm practice**
TRACK 38

EXERCISE 3
MEDIUM TEMPO RHYTHMIC PHRASING WITH INTERPRETATION – SWING

Now let's add interpretation to our rhythmic phrasing of "Dance with Me." Set your metronome to 150 bpm, then speak the lyric in time, testing many different rhythmic approaches to interpret the lyric. Repetition is key. While you may say the entire lyric over and over, it is often best to do each line several times before moving on. It's like "phrasing batting practice." You are researching the many ways you might deliver this lyric rhythmically and meaningfully. When you feel comfortable speaking the lyric in time with good interpretation options, apply some of your rhythmic ideas by singing the melody multiple times with the backing tracks (36/37). Take note of which ideas work well with the chords and which do not.

Here is an example of the first eight measures interpreted four different ways, followed by an entire chorus of interpreted rhythmic phrasing in a medium swing style. The goal words are in all caps. Reminder: At faster speeds, we will not necessarily identify a primary goal word and secondary goal word as we did with ballad singing. There is not as much time to spend on the various goal words.

Listen to Tracks 39 and 40 for demonstration.

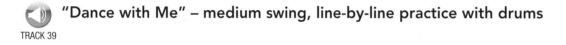

"Dance with Me" – medium swing, line-by-line practice with drums

TRACK 39

"Dance with Me" – medium swing, complete chorus with interpretation

TRACK 40

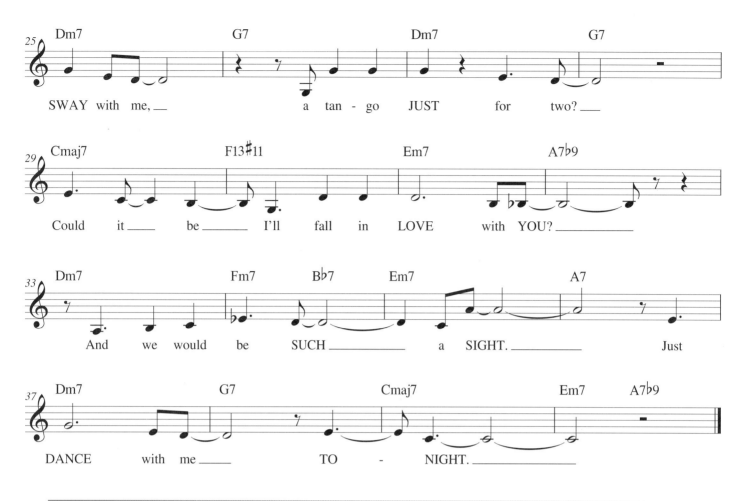

SWAY with me, ___ a tan - go JUST for two? ___ Could it ___ be ___ I'll fall in LOVE with YOU? ___ And we would be SUCH ___ a SIGHT. ___ Just DANCE with me ___ TO - NIGHT. ___

EXERCISE 4
UP-TEMPO RESTRICTIVE RHYTHM PRACTICE – SWING

Let's bump up the tempo! Set your metronome to 200 bpm or use the backing tracks for "Dance with Me" at a fast swing (41/42). Speak the lyric to "Dance with Me" using rhythmic phrasing, staying in-the-pocket 100 percent of the time. Get acquainted with the tempo, taking note of how a shorter, crisper speaking style makes delivering lyrics at this tempo a bit easier.

🔊 **"Dance with Me" – up-tempo swing, backing track (soprano key)**
TRACK 41

🔊 **"Dance with Me" – up-tempo swing, backing track (tenor/baritone key)**
TRACK 42

Next, as we did with our medium-swing version, let's explore rhythmic options at this tempo by speaking, and then singing, the song with the following rhythmic restrictions:

1. Quarter-Note Rhythms
The original melody contained mostly quarter-note rhythms, so in this exercise, let's change things up a bit. We want to use only quarter notes while sounding varied, yet natural. Here is an entire chorus of this rhythm to show how this might be done.

"Dance with Me" – up-tempo swing, quarter-note phrasing (alto key)

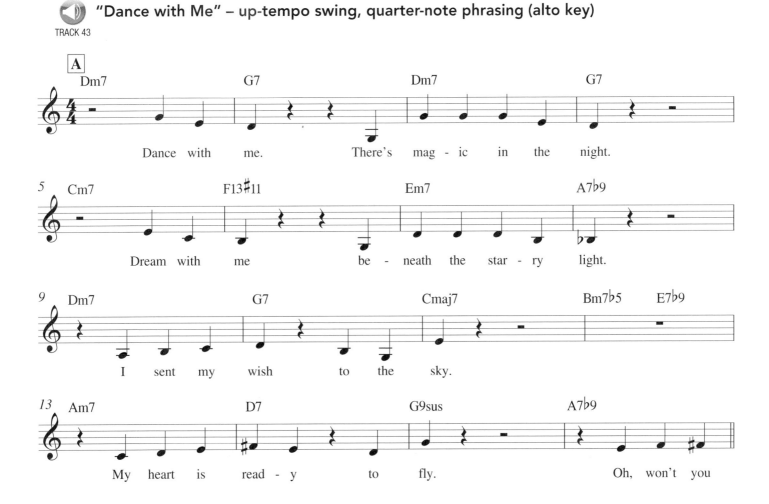

2. Syncopation

This syncopated version doesn't look exactly like the syncopated version we did in the medium-swing exercise. The increased speed can make consecutive syncopations sound frantic, so don't use too many in a row. The goal is simply to syncopate as frequently and naturally as this tempo will allow. (The carats indicate notes that are "off the beat.")

"Dance with Me" – up-tempo swing, syncopated phrasing

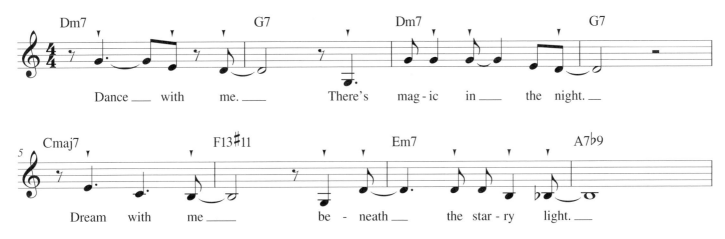

3. Dotted-Quarter Note (the hemiola effect)

This rhythm is a good choice for fast swing. When we use this pattern, the notes alternate between landing on a downbeat and landing on a syncopation. This gives our delivery a more relaxed feeling than consecutive syncopations. As an example, here is the second half of the song with the repeated dotted-quarter rhythm.

 **"Dance with Me"** – up-tempo swing, hemiola phrasing
TRACK 45

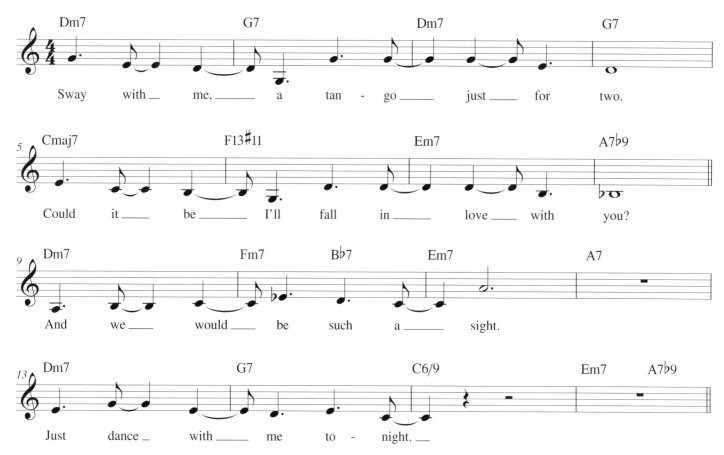

Get creative with the rhythmic restrictions you impose upon yourself. This will help you avoid habitual rhythmic patterns and discover other possibilities. Practicing one rhythmic concept at a time, as done in this exercise, will prove helpful when it comes time to interpret the lyric.

EXERCISE 5
APPLYING LYRIC INTERPRETATION – FAST SWING

Even though we are singing at a faster tempo, it is still possible (and important!) to add interpretation to the lyric. Take your lyric sheet and circle possible goal words. Again, you can stress goal words by holding them slightly longer or by singing them with more emphasis. Because the tempo is fast, we will not distinguish between primary and secondary goal words. Move less important words along more quickly to avoid getting too far behind in your phrasing. (For more detail on establishing goal words, see Chapter 1.)

Add interpretation to your delivery as you practice these three steps:

- Speak the lyrics rhythmically in a fast-swing style with a metronome at 200 bpm.
- Speak the lyrics to the backing tracks (41/42).
- Sing the lyrics to the backing tracks (41/42).

There are countless ways to phrase lyrics rhythmically, yet thoughtfully. On the following pages are four possible interpretations of the first 16 measures, with the intended goal words in all caps. The first four versions use one goal-word plan, and the second four versions use another goal-word plan.

To create varied approaches to goal words, I experimented quite a bit with the timing, sometimes arriving late to the phrase (back-phrasing), other times finishing a phrase early (front-phasing). Doing line-by-line "batting practice" with a metronome can unlock wonderful phrasing ideas. However, it's possible that not every rhythmic idea will fit with the chords of the song, so practice your ideas with a backing track to figure out which ideas work harmonically and which do not. In "Dance with Me," measure 8 has a tricky harmonic spot where the melody note lands on the ♭9 (a colorful altered note) of the chord. If I back-phrase too much, I'll clash with the chord before finally landing on the chord tone that fits. I have notated where there might be harmonic tension from this type of back-phrasing. On occasion, this can seem interesting, building a tension and release. At other times, it is just unpleasing to the ear. You be the judge!

"Dance with Me" – up-tempo swing, two sets of goal words, four ways each

🔊 **"Dance with Me" – fast swing, complete chorus with interpretation**

TRACK 47

Here is a complete chorus in a fast swing with interpretation for you to try.

EXERCISE 6
UP-TEMPO RHYTHM PRACTICE – SAMBA

Samba is a Brazilian genre of music. Its history is vast and deep. There are many types of samba grooves, but for the next three exercises we will focus on an up-tempo samba as played by many jazz artists today. "So Danco Samba" as performed by Eliane Elias or Antonio Carlos Jobim's "Samba Do Soho" are examples of this genre.

Here, we will mirror Exercise 4, this time with a samba feel. Using the samba backing tracks for "Dance with Me" (48/49), speak the lyric using rhythmic phrasing. The goal is to stay in-the-pocket 100 percent of the time, delivering the lyrics in a comfortable, confident, decisive manner. At this point, we are not necessarily trying to interpret the lyric. We are just getting acquainted with the tempo.

🔊 "Dance with Me" – up-tempo samba, 200 bpm, backing track (soprano key)

TRACK 48

🔊 "Dance with Me" – up-tempo samba, 200 bpm, backing track (tenor/baritone key)

TRACK 49

🔊 "Dance with Me" – up-tempo samba, 200 bpm, spoken lyric example

TRACK 50

Similar to Exercise 4, let's expand our rhythmic options with restrictive practice.

We can use the exact restrictions from Exercise 4:
- Quarter notes
- Syncopations
- Dotted-quarter notes (hemiola effect)

Look at the examples on page 25 and 26. We will speak and sing straight-eighth notes instead of swung-eighth notes; that's the only change to our delivery in the next three samba examples.

🔊 "Dance with Me" – up-tempo samba, 200 bpm, quarter-note phrasing (alto key)

TRACK 51

🔊 "Dance with Me" – up-tempo samba, 200 bpm, syncopation phrasing

TRACK 52

🔊 "Dance with Me" – up-tempo samba, 200 bpm, hemiola phrasing

TRACK 53

Get creative and use your own rhythmic restriction ideas. You want to be comfortable playing with the rhythmic phrasing of your lyric in different ways.

EXERCISE 7
APPLYING LYRIC INTERPRETATION – SAMBA

Repeat the steps in Exercise 5 of this chapter to add lyric interpretation to your samba rhythmic phrasing. Using Tracks 48 and 49, experiment with different combinations of goal words. All eight rhythmic delivery examples we used in Exercise 5 will work in a samba style as long as the eighth notes are not swung.

🔊 "Dance with Me" – up-tempo samba, 200 bpm, eight interpreted versions

TRACK 54

EXERCISE 8
SPONTANEITY PRACTICE

Take a short excerpt from a book and speak it to a fast tempo (170-200 bpm), with a particular groove in mind. Use a metronome, and strive to stay in-the-pocket the entire time. Do this over and over, varying the rhythmic placement. Aim for both meaning and rhythmic interest/style. Explore different styles as you do this (swing, samba, etc).

Need some inspiration? Ponder this excerpt from Paris Rutherford's book *The Vocal Jazz Ensemble*: "Interpreting music is a life-long pursuit; this is true in all styles. I believe a person grows into this ability over a long period of time – there are too many variables for it to come easily or quickly."

spontaneity practice, up-tempo

TRACK 55

BONUS EXERCISE
FAST SWING

Repeat exercises 6 and 7 at an even faster tempo for swing!
Use Tracks 57 and 58 as a sing-along at 300 bpm.

"Dance with Me" – fast swing, 300 bpm, phrasing example (alto key)

TRACK 56

"Dance with Me" – fast swing, 300 bpm, backing track (soprano key)

TRACK 57

"Dance with Me" – fast swing, 300 bpm, backing track (tenor/baritone key)

TRACK 58

CHAPTER 4
Exploring Other Grooves

Vocalists are often looking for ways to breathe new life into older songs. As a jazz singer, I frequently incorporate ballad, swing, and Brazilian styles when singing the Great American Songbook. However, I have found it fun to explore other grooves as a means of reinterpreting jazz standards. Whether you consider yourself a jazz singer, a pop singer, a cabaret singer, a folk singer, or just a singer of songs, the following five-step method can add adventure and variety to your set. In this chapter, we will explore cha-cha, mambo, reggae, back-beat grooves, double-time-feel grooves, and the odd meter grooves 7/4 and 5/4.

We will use "Dance with Me" for these groove exercises. Its simplicity makes the song a good candidate for groove experimentation. Rhythmically, the original melody utilizes only quarter notes, half notes, and whole notes, leaving lots of space for experimenting with rhythmic and phrasing. Harmonically, the tonal center does not shift quickly. Rather, it stays in the tonic key for long stretches at a time; this also allows for a lot of phrasing freedom. In terms of lyrics, the story is not emotionally deep. The topic is dancing, which potentially could fit any type of groove. If you haven't already, take time to learn "Dance with Me," researching the lyric and establishing goal words as described in Chapter 1.

As in Chapter 3, we will practice rhythmic phrasing from different angles. Since these grooves are not as commonly used in jazz and pop styles, we will employ a five-step process with each.

Five Steps to Thoughtful Rhythmic Phrasing in a New Groove

1. Researching the groove.
2. Trying it out: spoken, then sung with the backing track.
3. Rhythmic restrictions: spoken, then sung with the backing track.
4. Interpretation "batting practice": line-by-line repetition with metronome, varied each time.
5. Melody practice with new ideas.

EXERCISE 1
CHA-CHA

Step 1: Researching the Groove
The cha-cha is a dance and musical style originating in Cuba. Cha-cha is typically performed at a medium tempo to accommodate the cha-cha dance step, and the downbeats are emphasized. You will hear this pattern frequently in the percussion of a cha-cha:

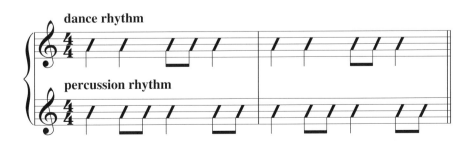

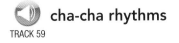
cha-cha rhythms
TRACK 59

If the band is playing "Dance with Me" with a cha-cha groove, we vocalists need to adjust our phrasing and tone to fit the new sound. Listen to traditional cha-cha music like "Oye Como Va," sung by famed Cuban singer Celia Cruz, to hear a great vocal model for both tone and phrasing of the cha-cha groove. These rhythms are found in the chorus of "Oye Como Va."

In "Oye Como Va," the melody is made of up strong downbeats and eighth-note groupings. When we sang "Dance with Me" as a medium swing or a bossa nova, it was fitting to use a great deal of syncopation since it is a dominant rhythmic element in both styles. In cha-cha, we'll focus on the downbeats and eighth-note groupings. We can still apply syncopation, but it won't be as constant as it was in swing and bossa nova.

Step 2: Trying It Out

Using the backing tracks (60/61) for "Dance with Me" in a cha-cha style, deliver the lyric, first spoken, then sung. Mimic the approach to rhythm and tone you heard while researching this style. Sing on downbeats, more than you did in the swing and samba styles.

🔊 "Dance with Me" – cha-cha, backing track (soprano key)
TRACK 60

🔊 "Dance with Me" – cha-cha, backing track (tenor/baritone key)
TRACK 61

Step 3: Rhythmic Restrictions

Here are two rhythmic restriction phrasing exercises for "Dance with Me" in a cha-cha style. They focus on the rhythms we heard during our research. You can speak or sing with the demo tracks or use the cha-cha backing track (60/61) to try the concepts on your own.

1. Sustained Downbeat Focus

In this first rhythmic restriction, we want to land on downbeats frequently, sustaining the downbeat pitch.

🔊 "Dance with Me" – cha-cha, sustained downbeats (alto key)
TRACK 62

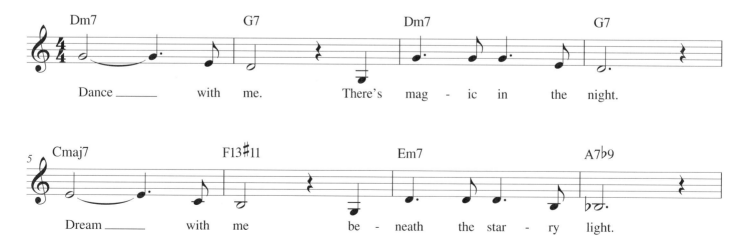

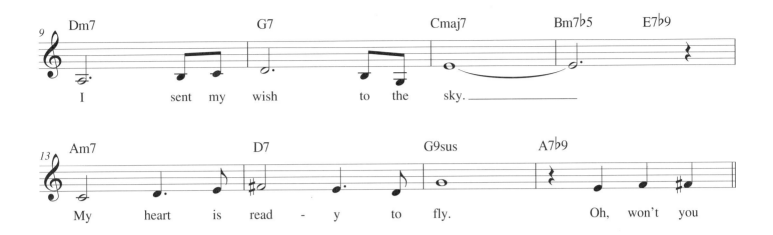

2. Back-phrasing to Create Eighth-Note Groupings

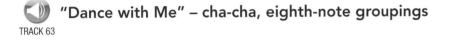 "Dance with Me" – cha-cha, eighth-note groupings

TRACK 63

Step 4: Interpretation "Batting Practice"

The following step can be done with a metronome, a groove app or groove software set to cha-cha, or the cha-cha drum track in Track 64 (removable vocal track on right side only). The tempo should be set to 130 bpm. (For more on "researching" your lyric to establish goal words, see Chapter 1.) The lyric should make sense while incorporating the downbeat emphasis and eighth-note groupings we just practiced. Emphasize goal words by holding them a bit longer or by stressing them more dynamically. In this style, you can also sing goal words as isolated short notes. As with other medium and fast styles, you might use only one goal word per phrase, as opposed to both primary and secondary goal words.

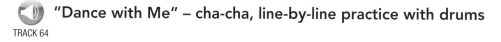 **"Dance with Me" – cha-cha, line-by-line practice with drums**
TRACK 64

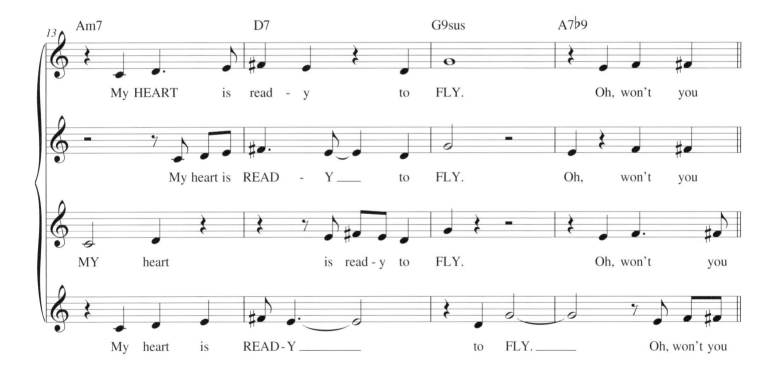

Step 5: Melody Practice with New Ideas

After rhythmic focus and repetitive interpretation practice, there should now be more information in your mental library. You have more ideas to draw on, so it's time to sing freely again, with no particular restrictions.

Here is an entire chorus with lyric interpretation, using the rhythmic ideas we practiced for a cha-cha style.

"Dance with Me" – cha-cha, complete chorus with interpretation

TRACK 65

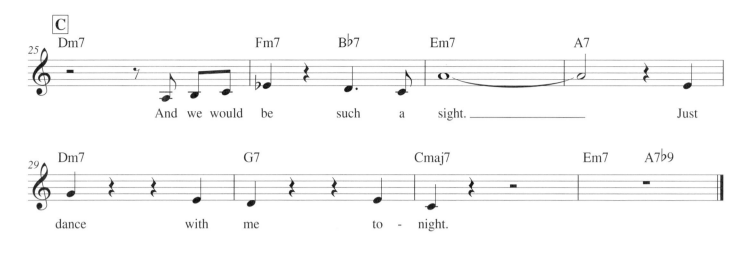

EXERCISE 2
MAMBO

Step 1: Researching the Groove

The mambo groove is a big sister to the cha-cha, with roots in Cuba and a strong history in areas like Puerto Rico and Mexico. Take time to explore recordings of traditional mambo grooves. One of my favorites is "Mambo Yo Yo," first recorded by Joe Arroyo. Ricardo Lemvo and Makina Loca later offered a slightly quicker tempo on the Putomayo CD *Afro Latino*. The mambo tempo is typically faster than cha-cha. Once you listen to some recordings of mambo, you'll find that syncopation is the significant rhythmic phrasing concept, different from the downbeat focus of the cha-cha.

Step 2: Trying It Out

After sampling several traditional mambo recordings, speak the lyric to "Dance with Me" as you listen to the mambo backing track for that song (66/67). When delivering the lyric, aim for three things:
* rhythmic phrasing, staying in-the-pocket at all times
* straight-eighth notes (not swung)
* frequent syncopation

We used frequent syncopation and a straight-eighth-note feel when we sang this song in a samba groove (Chapter 3).

"Dance with Me" – mambo, backing track (soprano key)

TRACK 66

"Dance with Me" – mambo, backing track (tenor/baritone key)

TRACK 67

Step 3: Rhythmic Restrictions

Using the mambo backing track, speak – then sing – the melody with the following rhythmic restrictions, two of which we used in the samba style.

1. Syncopations

"Dance with Me" – mambo, syncopation phrasing (alto key)
TRACK 68

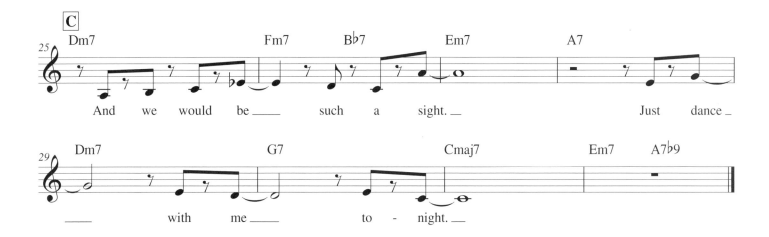

2. Dotted-quarter-note rhythm (hemiola effect)

"Dance with Me" – mambo, hemiola phrasing
TRACK 69

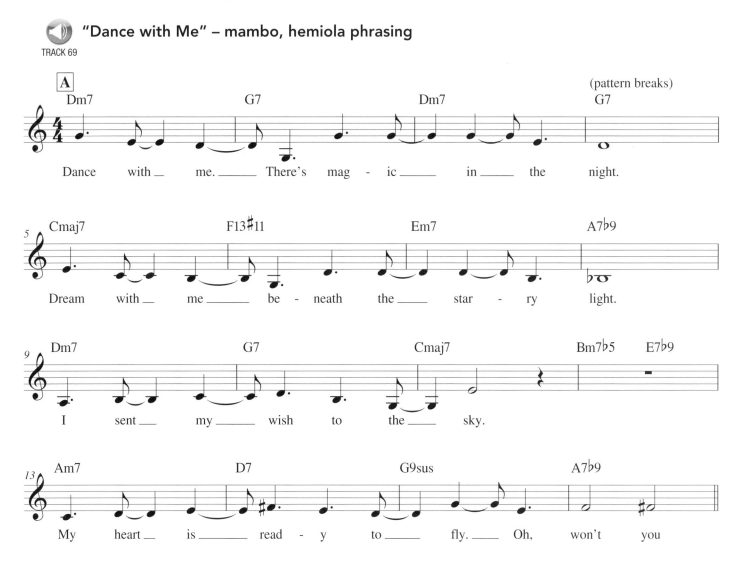

B

Dm7   G7   Dm7   G7

sway   with — me, —— a   tan - go —— just —— for   two?

Cmaj7   F13#11   Em7   A7♭9

Could   it —— be —— I'll   fall   in —— love — with   you?

C

Dm7   Fm7   B♭7   Em7   A7

And   we —— would —— be   such   a —— sight.

Dm7   G7   C6/9   Em7   A7♭9

Just   dance — with —— me   to - night. ——

Step 4: Interpretation "Batting Practice"

The following step can be done with a metronome, a groove app or groove software set to mambo, or the mambo drum track in Track 70 (removable vocal track on right side only). The tempo should be set to 200 bpm. Repeat each line many times before moving on to the next line, first speaking, then singing. Change the phrasing slightly each time, trying to honor goal words while still incorporating the syncopation concept. Experiment with different goal-word combinations, but be sure they make sense.

Version 1

DANCE with me. There's MAGIC in the night.
DREAM with me BENEATH the starry light.
I sent my WISH to the SKY.
My heart is READY to FLY.

Version 2

Dance with ME. There's magic in the NIGHT.
DREAM with me beneath the STARRY light.
I SENT my wish to the SKY.
My HEART is ready to FLY.

These goal-word plans could be rhythmically interpreted like this:

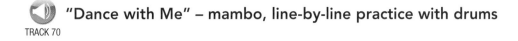

"Dance with Me" – mambo, line-by-line practice with drums

TRACK 70

Step 5: Melody Practice with New Ideas

After all that focused practice, surely there are lots of ideas in your mental library. Let's try them out!
Sing "Dance with Me" in its entirety several times, incorporating the new concepts you have uncovered in
your detailed practice.

Here is an entire chorus of "Dance with Me" interpreted in a mambo style. Memorizing this
interpretation will help pave the way to even greater creativity.

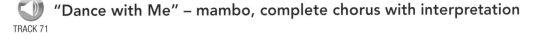

"Dance with Me" – mambo, complete chorus with interpretation

TRACK 71

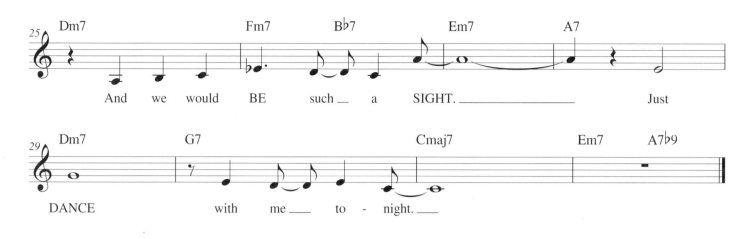

And we would BE such a SIGHT. _____ Just DANCE with me ___ to - night. ___

EXERCISE 3
BACK-BEAT SWUNG-16TH STYLES
(R&B, FUNK, HIP-HOP, ET AL.)

Step 1: Research the Groove

In today's music scene, there are many genres, and blends thereof, that include back-beat-style drumming (emphasizing beats 2 and 4) while incorporating an underlying subdivision of swinging 16th notes. Because they share the element of the swing-feel, these types of grooves work well as backdrops for jazz swing tunes. With so many grooves and groove-blends in this category, we won't get into the intricacies and vocal traditions of each one; that would fill another book entirely! Rather, let's focus on an R&B groove inspired by songs like "Mornin'" by jazz vocalist Al Jarreau and "India Arie" by R&B vocalist India Arie. Take time to listen to these songs. Notice the strong downbeat on beat 1 and the many syncopations after.

The tempo of this R&B groove feels like it is about 90 bpm. We have been singing "Dance with Me" at 150 bpm for medium swing and 200 bpm for fast swing. Slowing down to 90 bpm will feel very different. So, if we want to aim for the same type of groove we heard in "Mornin'" and "India Arie," we have two options:

1. Slow the tempo to 90 bpm. The band will groove well at this tempo, and our melody will move slowly over the top of it, probably utilizing much more sustain.

2. Have the band play at 180 bpm while incorporating a "half-time feel:" They will read the music at 180 bpm, but will play with the "feel" as though it were 90 bpm. Listen to Track 72 to hear the difference.

🔊 **"Dance with Me" – 90 bpm vs. 180 bpm half-time feel**
TRACK 72

Here is what the back-beat notation looks like for both of these options.

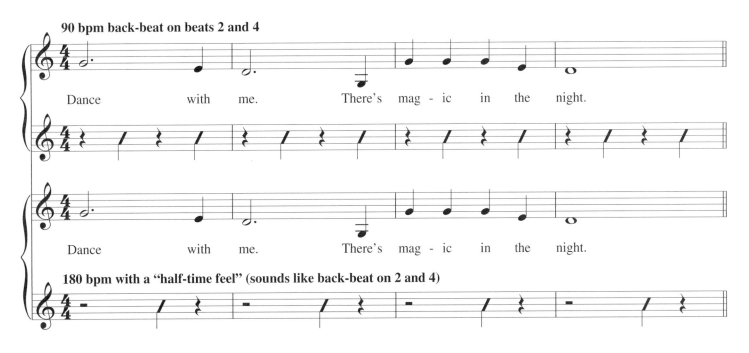

90 bpm back-beat on beats 2 and 4

Dance with me. There's mag - ic in the night.

Dance with me. There's mag - ic in the night.

180 bpm with a "half-time feel" (sounds like back-beat on 2 and 4)

Step 2: Trying It Out

After listening to recordings for inspiration, speak – then sing – the lyric to "Dance with Me" using the R&B backing track (73/74). See what comes naturally to your phrasing, taking note of how much downbeat emphasis vs. syncopation you naturally feel inclined to do.

🔊 **"Dance with Me" – R&B, backing track (soprano key)**
TRACK 73

🔊 **"Dance with Me" – R&B, backing track (tenor/baritone key)**
TRACK 74

Step 3: Rhythmic Restrictions

Again, this R&B groove is a back-beat style that, like funk, welcomes melodies with a strong beat-1 downbeat and lots of syncopation in between. (Note: With faster grooves like an up-tempo funk, the beat-1 downbeat might only be emphasized every two measures.)

For our restrictive rhythm exercise, let's incorporate downbeats with syncopation in between. Speak, then sing, the following example.

"Dance with Me" – R&B, spoken, then sung (alto key)

Other restrictive rhythm practice possibilities include:
- Syncopation (no downbeat emphasis)
- Quarter notes (no syncopation)
- Hemiola (repeated dotted-quarter notes)

We used the above restrictions on pages 25 and 26. You can read along with those restrictive rhythm exercises while using the R&B backing tracks.

Step 4: Interpretation "Batting Practice"

Set your metronome to 90 bpm – or 180 if you prefer to divide the beat. It's time for our line-by-line repetitive goal-word practice. Using the options below or your own, repeat each line a number of times. Explore the various ways you can bring out the goal words while incorporating the rhythmic concepts we just practiced.

DANCE with me. There's MAGIC in the night.
DREAM with me BENEATH the starry light.
I sent my WISH to the SKY.
My heart is READY to FLY.

Oh, won't you SWAY with me, a TANGO just for two?
Could it BE I'll FALL in love with you?
And we would be SUCH a SIGHT.
Just DANCE with me TONIGHT.

To get you started, here are two different interpretations of the first 16 bars, using the goal-word emphasis above.

"Dance with Me" – R&B, line-by-line practice with drums

TRACK 76

Step 5: Melody Practice with New Ideas

Let's put our hard work to the test! Sing through the melody in its entirety again, using the R&B backing track. By now, you will have uncovered new ways to emphasize the goal words of your song, while also incorporating the R&B rhythms we practiced. If you still don't feel comfortable creating your own phrasing in this style, or any of the styles, memorize the interpreted chorus provided in Step 5 of each exercise in this chapter. While you don't want that to be your only set of interpretation ideas, it will jump-start your mental library.

🔊 **"Dance with Me" – R&B, complete chorus with interpretation**
TRACK 77

EXERCISE 4
REGGAE

Step 1: Researching the Groove

Reggae is a groove that originated in Jamaica. Bob Marley was one of the most famous reggae artists of all time; we will use his version of "Three Little Birds" as our inspiration for this exercise. Take time to listen to "Three Little Birds," as well as many other Bob Marley songs, to get the sound and feel of authentic reggae in your ear. Listen to the bass, drums, and guitar. As with the R&B groove from the previous example, reggae is typically played with a relaxed quarter-note tempo, incorporating back-beats on 2 and 4. The 16th-note subdivision has a little swing to it, but the amount of swing varies. Some musicians play with a straighter feel, while others swing harder.

Let's take a look at some of the rhythms in Bob Marley's "Three Little Birds." The example on page 54 is written in the slow reggae tempo, not the half-time feel we will use with our jazz song. In a reggae groove, the guitar or piano customarily plays off-beats, either an eighth note or two 16ths. We hear strong downbeats on beat 1 in the bass. (Take note of another type of bass line on the next page.) The vocal rhythms also use strong downbeats, and everyone locks in with the three layers of subdivision at one point or another. Notice the minimal usage of sustained pitch in the vocal line; many notes are delivered with a short release. In Step 3, we will look at this in more detail.

"Three Little Birds"

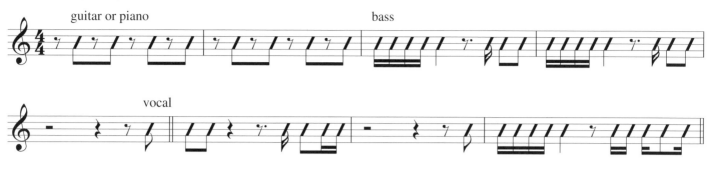

Here's another comping rhythm for reggae:

Many jazz songs transfer well to a reggae groove; it's fun to put it to use on a gig as a way to vary a performance set. As in the previous etude, you have two options with this type of relaxed groove: 1) sing the melody at half the speed; 2) have the band play regular speed, but with a half-time feel. The second option is the more common, and it is how we will approach this exercise. Refer to Exercise 3 for more detail on half-time feel.

Step 2: Trying It Out

After listening to recordings of traditional reggae for inspiration, speak – then sing – the lyric to "Dance with Me" while listening to the reggae (half-time feel) backing track (78/79). See what comes naturally to your phrasing, taking note of how you are adjusting your rhythms to fit the slower tempo and the underlying swing feel.

🔊 **"Dance with Me" – reggae, backing track (soprano key)**
TRACK 78

🔊 **"Dance with Me" – reggae, backing track (tenor/baritone key)**
TRACK 79

Step 3: Rhythmic Restrictions

For our rhythmic restrictions, we'll explore three layers of subdivision, notated in a half-time feel. We will also incorporate the short-note style prevalent in reggae. Speak – then sing – "Dance with Me," using only written half notes and quarter notes. Don't sustain beyond those note values; keep the notes short. Note: Because of the half-time feel, the quarter notes will feel like eighth notes.

🔊 **"Dance with Me" – reggae, quarter notes and half notes (alto key)**
TRACK 80

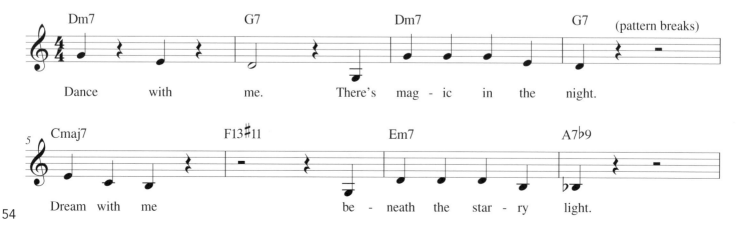

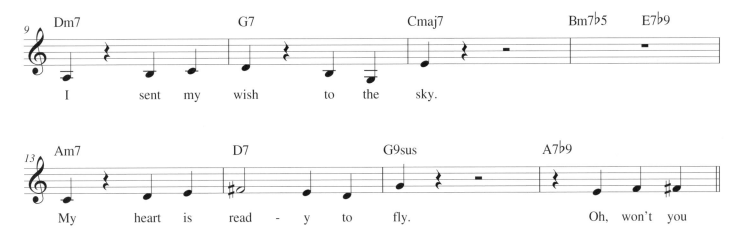

To catch the next layer of subdivision, speak – then sing – "Dance with Me," using groups of lightly swung eighth notes. (Listen to Bob Marley recordings to get the swing style in your ear.) Use at least two eighths at a time. You will need to back-phrase (delay phrase entrance) quite a bit to use this rhythm exclusively. Here is an example:

"Dance with Me" – reggae, swung eighth notes (which feel like 16th notes)

TRACK 81

Step 4: Interpretation "Batting Practice"

The following step can be done with a metronome, a groove app or groove software set to reggae, or the reggae drum track in Track 82 (removable vocal track on right side only). The tempo should be set to 72 bpm (or 144 if you prefer to subdivide the beat). Repeat each line several times, exploring the various rhythmic ways you can interpret the lyrics. (You're likely now a pro at this if you have used this book in sequence!) This melody doesn't have a lot of words, so there will likely be a lot of space in your delivery. This makes for a fun challenge! Even though we are not sustaining notes as much in this style, we might bring out goal words by putting them on downbeats, singing them as short solitary notes, holding them for a bit more time, or simply emphasizing them dynamically with our voices. Continue to focus on thoughtful goal words, aiming for many different interpretations.

Dance with me. There's magic in the night.
Dream with me beneath the starry light.
I sent my wish to the sky.
My heart is ready to fly.

Oh, won't you sway with me, a tango just for two?
Could it be I'll fall in love with you?
And we would be such a sight.
Just dance with me tonight.

Here are two different interpretations of the first 16 bars to get you started.

"Dance with Me" – reggae, line-by-line practice with drums

TRACK 82

Step 5: Melody Practice with New Ideas

Let's see if all that targeted practice has helped us develop new ideas. Sing through the melody in its entirety again several times, using the reggae backing track. Try to make each chorus a little different. The goal is to have practiced many phrasing options that are connected to both the rhythmic style and the lyric.

Here is an example of an entire chorus interpreted in the reggae style.

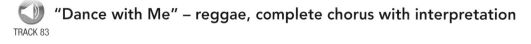

"Dance with Me" – reggae, complete chorus with interpretation

TRACK 83

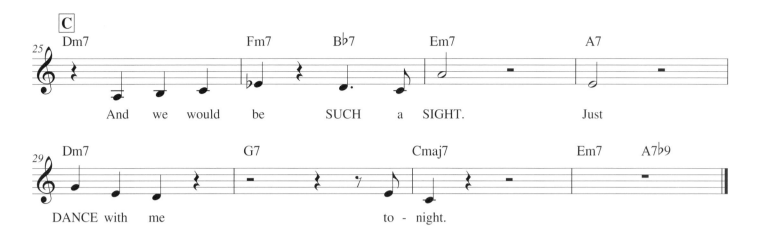

And   we   would   be   SUCH   a   SIGHT.   Just

DANCE with   me   to - night.

EXERCISE 5
7/4 (4+3)

Step 1: Researching the Groove

This example employs an R&B half-time-feel groove similar to the one in Exercise 3, but we'll change the time signature to 7/4 time. When we deal with odd meters that have more than four beats to the bar, it is common to divide the beats into smaller groups. For example, in grooves with 7/4 time or 7/8 time, we can feel the groove as four beats plus three beats – or three beats plus four beats.

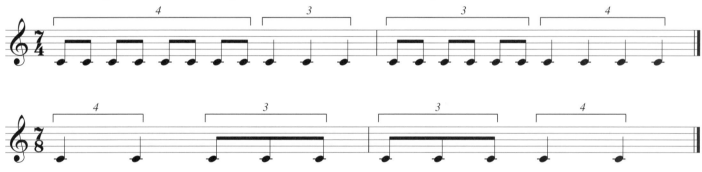

In 9/8 time, we could feel it as 3+3+3, 5+4, 4+5, or any other combination. Usually, the start of each new smaller group in the bar sounds like a mini-downbeat in the measure, so breaking down the feel can help get everyone on the same "accent page." Note: When we take pieces originally in 4/4 time and convert them to be performed in an odd meter, it is important to experiment with different meters and internal subdivisions to find the most natural choice.

To get an idea of what this type of meter and subdivision sounds like, take a listen to:
- "It Might as Well Be Spring" (by Rodgers and Hammerstein), as performed by pianist Brad Mehldau
  Note: Melody begins at 0:31
- "Overjoyed" (by Stevie Wonder), as performed by pianist Danilo Perez
  Note: Bridge is in 3/4 time
- "Golden Lady" (by Stevie Wonder), as performed by singer Kurt Elling

For this exercise, we will keep the same general quarter-note tempo for "Dance with Me," delivering the melody in 7/4 time. Note: We are not making every 4/4 measure into a 7/4 measure. Rather, we are spreading the 7/4 over two measures. What results is the sense that we are singing in 4/4 time, but with a beat missing every other bar. It will feel like this:

Step 2: Trying It Out

This groove might be unfamiliar to you, but just dig in. Speak, then sing, through the song with the 7/4 backing track. Take note of any pitfalls in the lyric where you might need to work out the phrasing.

🔊 "Dance with Me" – 7/4 time, backing track (soprano key)
TRACK 84

🔊 "Dance with Me" – 7/4 time, backing track (tenor/baritone key)
TRACK 85

Step 3: Rhythmic Restrictions

Using the backing track for "Dance with Me" in 7/4 time, try the following two rhythmic restriction exercises. The first etude aims to land on beats 1, 3, 5, and 6½ as much as possible, like this:

🔊 "Dance with Me" – 7/4 time, emphasizing internal downbeats (alto key)
TRACK 86

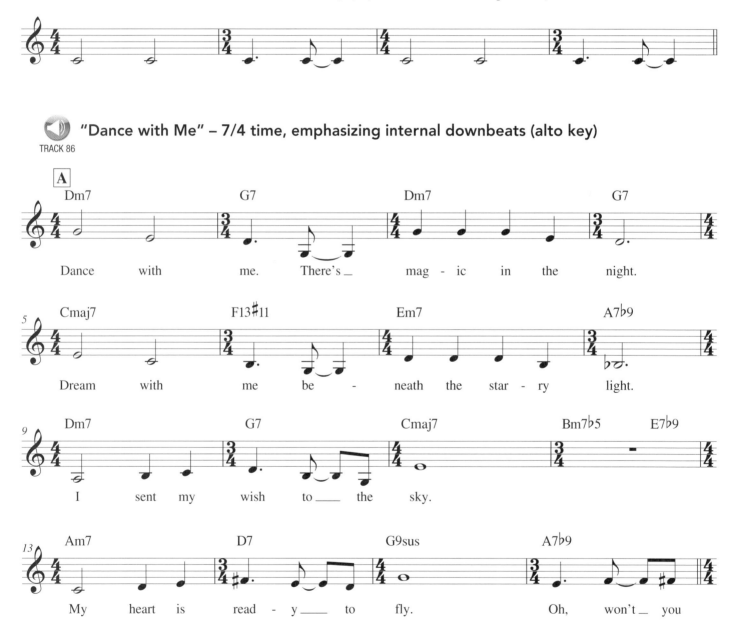

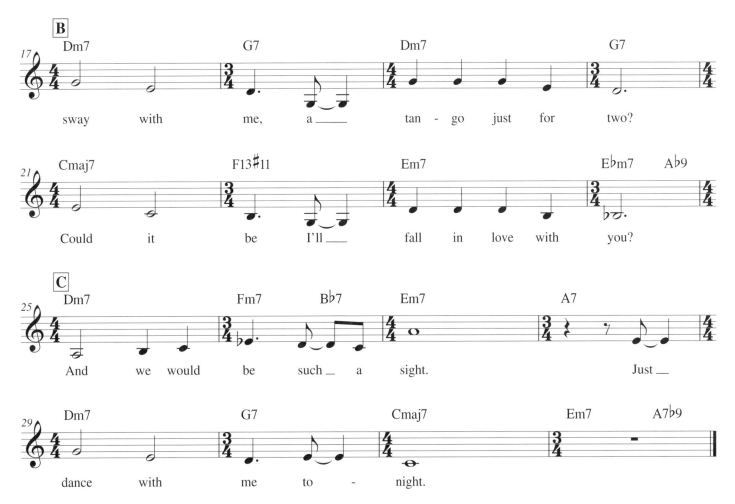

The second rhythmic restriction incorporates back-phrasing (delaying each entrance). Avoid the downbeat of the 4/4 measure while clearly landing on the downbeat of the 3/4 measure.

"Dance with Me" – 7/4 time, delayed entrances
TRACK 87

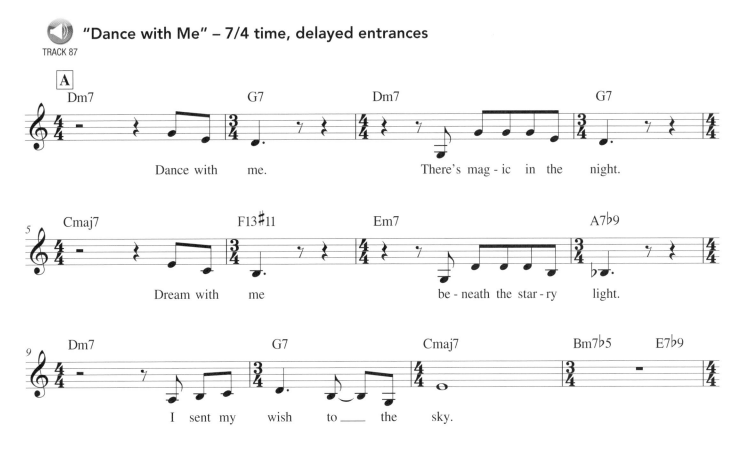

Step 4: Interpretation "Batting Practice"

It's time for our line-by-line repetitive goal word practice. Using the goal-word options below, repeat each line numerous times, exploring the many ways you can vary the rhythm delivery. Remember: We are trying to make the lyrics sound natural and meaningful, even while negotiating this odd meter. This exercise can be done with a metronome, a groove app or groove software set to 7/4 time, or the 7/4 drum track in track 88 (removable vocal track on right side only). The tempo should be set to 156 bpm.

Here are two different interpretations of the first 16 bars, with goal words in caps.

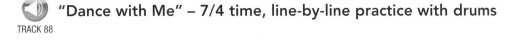

"Dance with Me" – 7/4 time, line-by-line practice with drums

TRACK 88

Step 5: Melody Practice with New Ideas

Your mental library is filling with new ideas. Let's put them to the test. Sing through the melody in its entirety multiple times, using the 7/4 backing track. Strive to make each chorus slightly different. Our aim is to use some of our rhythmic ideas, as well as to acknowledge goal words.

Here is an example of an entire chorus interpreted in a 7/4 style. (I experimented with a few different goal words.)

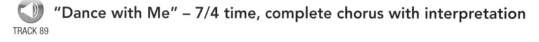

"Dance with Me" – 7/4 time, complete chorus with interpretation

TRACK 89

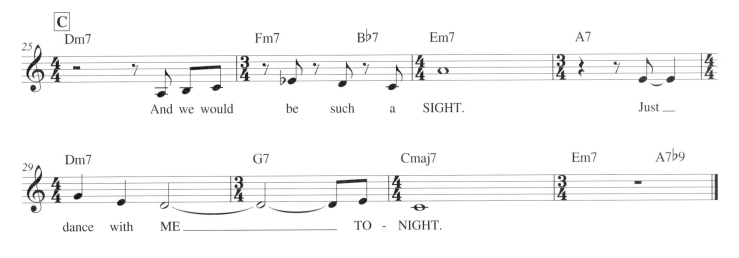

And we would be such a SIGHT. Just ___ dance with ME _____ TO - NIGHT.

EXERCISE 6
5/4 (3+2)

Step 1: Researching the Groove

Many songs originally in 4/4 time can easily be transferred to 5/4 or 5/8 time. That sort of meter change can breathe new life into a song's interpretation. For these exercises, we will employ a 3+2 subdivision. Generally, this will cause the groove to feel like a waltz with a beat missing in every other bar.

To get a feeling for the sound of 5/4 time, take a listen to the following recordings of two of my former students from the University of North Texas. (I love these performances!)

- "What'll I Do" (Irving Berlin), sung by Hildegunn Gjedrem
- "Glitter in the Air" (Pink/Billy Mann), sung by Sarah Kervin

and also…

- "I Didn't Know What Time it Was" (Rodgers and Hart), played by renowned jazz pianist Brad Mehldau

Step 2: Trying It Out

"Dance with Me" works quite well in 5/4 time. We can replace each 4/4 measure with a measure of 5/4 by adding one beat to each bar. This allows us further time to deliver the lyric. "Dance with Me" naturally has a nice bit of space; adding even more will feel comfortable as long as the tempo isn't too slow. We'll use a measure subdivision of 3+2. The change in time looks like this:

Using the backing track, speak – then sing – through the song in 5/4 time. Feel the 3+2 subdivision as you sing. Take note of any pitfalls in the lyric where you might need to work out the phrasing.

🔊 "Dance with Me" – 5/4 time, backing track (soprano key)
TRACK 90

🔊 "Dance with Me" – 5/4 time, backing track (tenor/baritone key)
TRACK 91

Step 3: Rhythmic Restrictions

Using the backing track in 5/4, speak – then sing – through the following rhythmic restriction exercises. Remember that we are not necessarily concentrating on goal words or interpretation during these exercises. We are simply exploring our rhythmic options.

First, let's focus on sustained downbeats. We are aiming to land on the downbeat, sustain for the majority of the measure, and sing quick pickups into the next bar. Here is an example of the first 16 measures of the song with this rhythmic restriction.

🔊 "Dance with Me" – 5/4 time, sustained downbeats (alto key)
TRACK 92

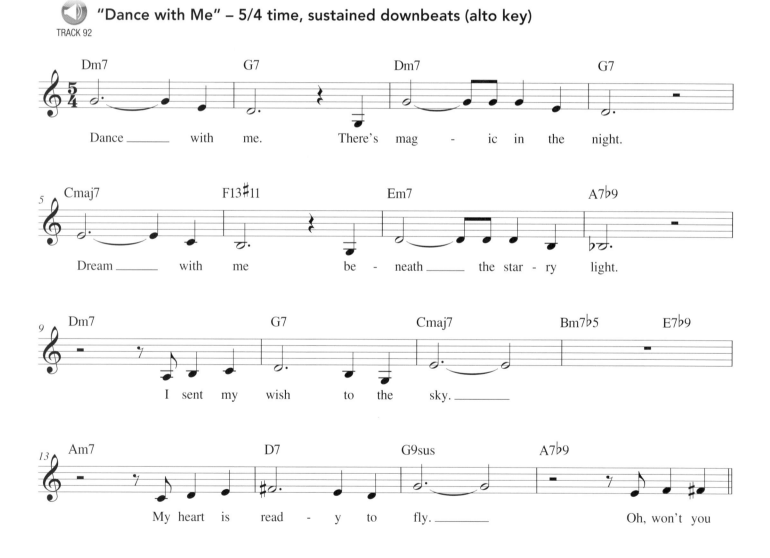

Next, let's focus on singing two dotted-quarter notes at the start of the measure.

TRACK 93 **"Dance with Me" – 5/4 time, dotted-quarter notes**

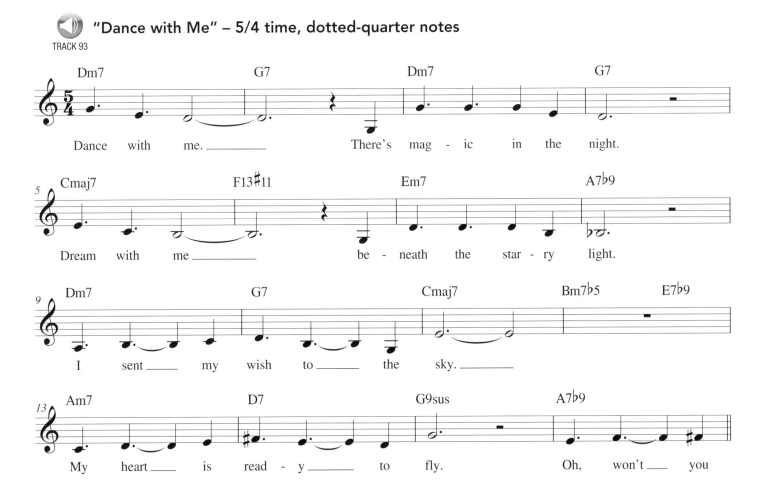

Step 4: Interpretation "Batting Practice"

As with the other grooves, we'll do line-by-line repetitive goal-word practice to explore rhythm interpretation options and quicken our interpretation reflexes. Goal words can be emphasized by placing them on downbeats, holding them longer, or simply giving them more vocal dynamic or inflection.

This exercise can be done with a metronome (175 bpm set to 5/4 time), a groove app or groove software, or the 5/4 drum track in Track 94 (removable vocal track on right side only). Now repeat each line many times; with each reiteration, try to incorporate a different goal-word plan.

Here are four combinations of two different lines from "Dance with Me."

(two short phrases – one goal word each)
Dance with ME. There's MAGIC in the night.
DANCE with me. There's magic in the NIGHT.
Dance with ME. There's magic in the NIGHT.
DANCE with me. There's MAGIC in the night.

(one long phrase – two goal words)
I sent my WISH to the sky.
I SENT my WISH to the sky.
I sent my WISH to the SKY.
I sent MY wish to the SKY.

Rhythmically, those options might look like this:

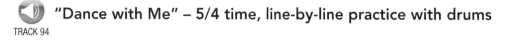

"Dance with Me" – 5/4 time, line-by-line practice with drums

TRACK 94

Step 5: Melody Practice with New Ideas

It's time to put our preparation to the test! Sing through the melody in its entirety many times, using the 5/4 backing track. Hopefully you have uncovered new ways to emphasize the goal words of your song, while also incorporating the rhythms we practiced. If you still don't feel comfortable coming up with your own phrasing in this style, or any of the styles, memorize the interpreted chorus provided in Step 5 of each exercise in this chapter. While you don't want that to be your only set of interpretation ideas, it will jump-start your mental library.

"Dance with Me" – 5/4 time, complete chorus with interpretation

EXERCISE 7
DOUBLE-TIME-FEEL SWING

Step 1: Research the Groove

Setting songs to a double-time-feel swing or samba groove can breathe new life into a standard song you have been singing for years. Let's make a distinction between the terms *double-time* and *double-time-feel*. First, double-time means the quarter-note speed will literally double the original speed. If you began singing "Dance with Me" at ♩ = 90, switching to double-time would mean suddenly singing it at 180 bpm. A double-time-feel, however, is a groove that feels like you are performing at 180 bpm, but the quarter note actually remains at 90. (Listen to the explanation of double-time feel on Track 96.)

🔊 **"Dance with Me" – double-time-feel swing, explanation**
TRACK 96

The difference looks like this:

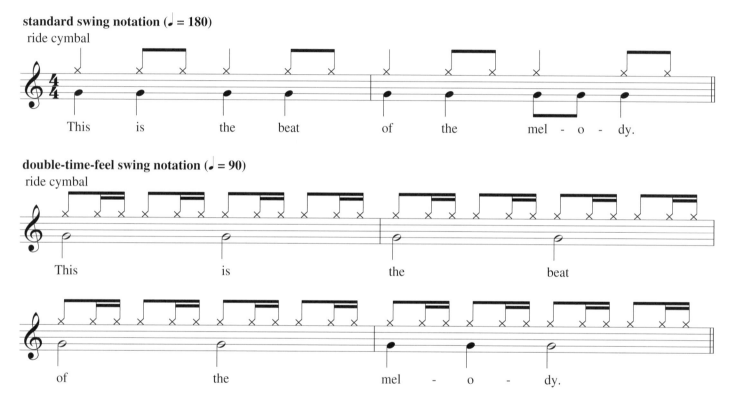

Step 2: Try It

Double-time feel is often used by singers when they want the feeling of a fast tempo, but don't wish to sing the melody quickly. If the tempo is 130 bpm, but the band plays with a double-time feel, the tempo will feel like 260 bpm. Sing "Dance with Me" with the backing track in a double-time-feel swing style.

🔊 **"Dance with Me" – double-time-feel swing, backing track (soprano key)**
TRACK 97

🔊 **"Dance with Me" – double-time-feel swing, backing track (tenor/baritone key)**
TRACK 98

Step 3: Rhythmic Restrictions

From a vocal standpoint, the melody is actually moving at a rather slow and calm pace, while the band is playing with a lot of energy. It is a good idea to try and embrace both the calm of the drawn-out melody, as well as the energy of the band.

Our first rhythmic restriction exercise in this style focuses on two elements. First, we will practice singing with a lot of sustain, to fill up more space. Second, we will use syncopation to lock in with the style of the band. Using one syncopated note toward the end of a phrase usually does the trick. You need not syncopate many notes in a row. In fact, singing with many repeated syncopations at this tempo with a swing feel can sometimes feel frantic. Note: To meet up with the syncopation style of the band in this double-time feel, we will need to syncopate at the 16th-note subdivision level. Try these phrases with the backing track and continue the concept for the rest of the song.

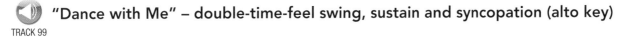

"Dance with Me" – double-time-feel swing, sustain and syncopation (alto key)
TRACK 99

Our next rhythmic restriction exercise will focus on front-loading the phrases with quarter notes. Remember that our tempo is 130 bpm, so the quarter notes will seem rather slow compared to the feeling of the track.

"Dance with Me" – double-time-feel swing, quarter-note front phrasing

TRACK 100

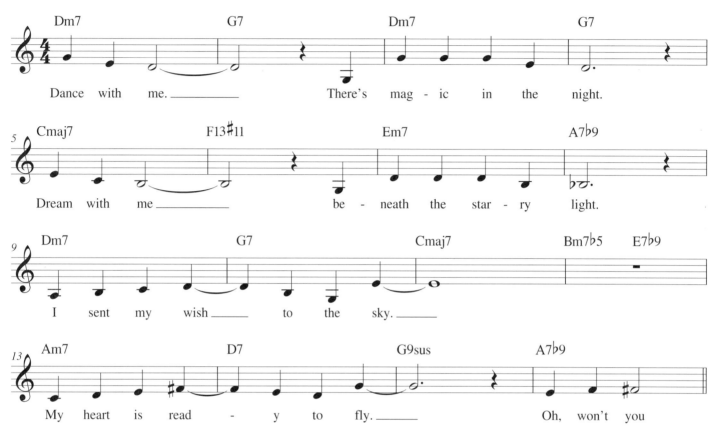

Step 4: Interpretation "Batting Practice"

You can do this step with a metronome, a groove app or groove software set to swing, or the double-time-feel drum track in Track 101 (removable vocal track on right side only). The tempo should be set to 260 bpm, but think of the beats as eighth notes. We are in a double-time feel, so the quarter notes will be moving relatively slowly. Isolate each line, repeating it many times. Think of possible goal-word combinations. Experiment with various ways of targeting goal words while incorporating floating sustained sounds, occasional syncopations, and front-loading quarter notes as we did in our rhythmic exercises.

Here are the first 16 measures, with each line interpreted three ways.

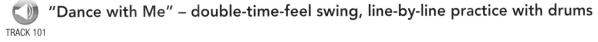

"Dance with Me" – double-time-feel swing, line-by-line practice with drums
TRACK 101

Step 5: Melody Practice with New Ideas

You have some new ideas to try out. Sing through "Dance with Me" in its entirety multiple times, incorporating your newly uncovered phrasing options.

Here is an entire chorus of "Dance with Me," interpreted in a double-time-feel swing. If you still aren't comfortable singing or interpreting lyrics in this style, remember that repeating and memorizing these exercises will fill your mental library with a lot of phrasing vocabulary. In time, you will feel more fluent in each of these grooves.

"Dance with Me" – double-time-feel swing, complete chorus with interpretation

TRACK 102

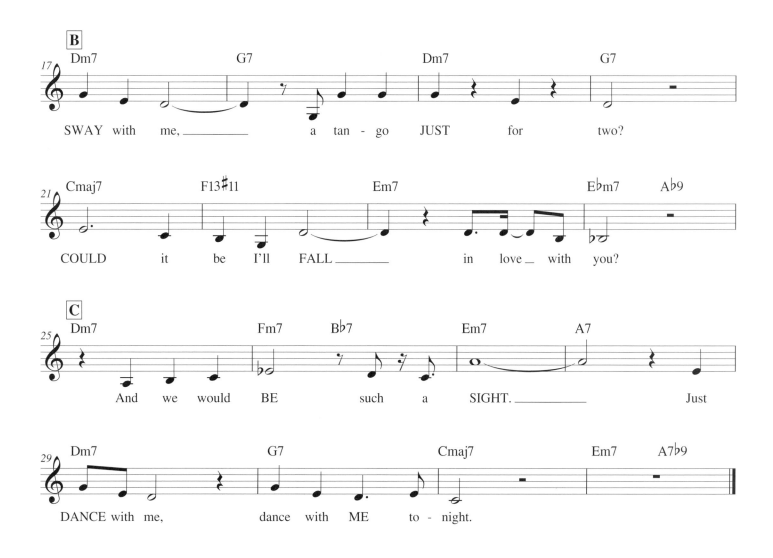

BONUS STEP

You can also try singing this song as a samba with a double-time feel. Singing some nice sustained notes is still a good idea; however, you can further experiment with consecutive syncopations in samba because the eighth notes are not swung. This makes it easier and less frantic to sing repeated syncopations. Listen to an example of "Dance with Me" sung this way, then use Tracks 104/105 for your samba double-time-feel backing tracks

"Dance with Me" – double-time-feel samba, example (alto key)

TRACK 103

"Dance with Me" – double-time-feel samba, backing track (soprano key)

TRACK 104

"Dance with Me" – double-time-feel samba, backing track (tenor/baritone key)

TRACK 105

SECTION 2
Tone:
Color It Like You Say It

CHAPTER 5
Vocal Technique Basics

Great vocal technique = confidence and creative freedom! Developing and maintaining superior vocal technique is a lifelong journey. The best storytellers explore their vocal expression, dynamic range, tone colors, and vocal range. If we as *singing* storytellers are not secure with our vocal technique, it can hinder our ability to relate with confidence the story we want to tell.

For the sake of continuity, the various components of this chapter are separated into individual exercises. However, they are truly lifelong pursuits. These skills take time to develop, and once developed, they must be practiced regularly in order to maintain the skill.

EXERCISE 1
BREATH MANAGEMENT

When we exhale naturally, in a relaxed state, the breath flows out rather quickly and uneventfully. When we sing, however, we are releasing the air at a much slower rate. Something in our body has to control how much air comes out when we sing and at what speed, keeping it steady as it is released. We call this *breath management*. The establishment of proper breath management is the most significant element to a solid singing technique. While it is natural for beginning singers to want to manage the breath in their throats, which is often what we do when we speak, it is important to establish subglottal (below the vocal cords) breath management. This will keep the vocal cords free to produce sound easily and efficiently.

Try these exercises to understand the feeling of proper breath support.

1. Hissing: Stand tall, with good posture and your sternum lifted. Take a deep breath through your nose. Feel your ribs expand outward. Exhale. Feel them return to their starting position. Breathe deeply through the nose again, once again noting the expanding ribcage. On the exhale, hiss ("ssssss") at a medium-loud volume using moderately fast airspeed. As you do this, keep your ribcage out, expanded. Notice how the abdominal muscles have to engage in order to keep the ribs from falling back to the starting position. It should not feel tense, simply engaged. As you hiss, be aware that your throat is not engaged; it is impossible for it to engage while hissing. This hissing exercise simulates singing with proper breath support.

2. In, Hold, Out: Still with good posture, breathe in slowly for ten seconds. Hold your breath for ten seconds with your throat open and ribcage expanded. (Do not put your vocal folds together; your throat should feel open, as though you are about to say "hi.") Then, exhale for ten seconds while hissing. This exercise can be done with five-second increments or up to 15 seconds. It is a way to become familiar with the coordination of singing without using unhealthy throat tension as a form of breath management.

3. Slow, Hot-Air Exhale: As you stand up straight, breathe in slowly through your mouth. Exhale slow, hot air, as though you are warming your hands gradually with your breath. Use the syllable "hoh," but make the sound completely silent. You shouldn't make any noise with your throat. Go as slowly as you can. Then, increase the air speed. Notice the subglottal activity. In other words, feel your abs at work, your ribcage muscles keeping the ribs in that expanded position. This gentle, engaged abdominal feeling is what you want to aim for when you sing.

EXERCISE 2
THE SOFT PALATE

Understanding how to raise and lower the soft palate will have a tremendous effect on your ability to adjust your tone, intonation, and volume. Soft palate control can also play a big part in shifting between vocal registers and navigating the entire vocal range smoothly.

1. Where is it?: The roof of your mouth is your hard palate. The soft palate is the soft tissue you can feel with your tongue at the back of your hard palate. Hold your nose shut and pop your ears, as you might do on an airplane to unstop them. The soft palate usually goes up all the way when we do this. The soft palate also lifts when we yawn. (You might be yawning right now!) Try to speak with the soft palate lifted as high as it can go. Notice how it changes the sound of your voice.

2. Muh, muh, muh: Start with your soft palate lowered, in a resting position, likely where it is when you speak. Start saying the syllable "muh." As you repeat this word, lift your soft palate. Try to go from a flat soft palate to a totally lifted soft palate and back down to flat in one breath.

🔊 soft palate discovery exercise
TRACK 106

3. Speaking/singing experiments: Recite this lyric over and over, striving to change the size of your sound by raising the soft palate: "I had always wanted someone to love. Then suddenly, you appeared."

    Establish what it feels like to speak with varying degrees of lift. Aim for at least five different soft palate settings. Then sing the words on a comfortable note or set of notes with the same five settings of soft-palate lift. You will notice that, by lifting the palate even a little, the placement of the vocal sound seems to move higher in the head. A flat soft palate often leads to the sound of the voice resonating in the throat, while a lifted palate moves the resonance to a higher (and healthier!) place.

🔊 soft palate speaking, varying lifts
TRACK 107

4. Exploring resonance: Speak the lyrics from Step 3 again, this time aiming your sound into your nose. It should sound like a forward placement, even whiny. Recite it again and aim the sound toward the back of your mouth. Do this with your soft palate up and then repeat with it lowered. Sometimes it is helpful to assign names to these different sounds (e.g., a lowered soft palate aimed to the back of the mouth is a "Kermit the Frog" sound). Naming these placements helps us find them later, when we need them.

5. Tonal practice, speaking: Recite the lyric below many times, using one of the following approaches with each repetition.

    "I had always wanted someone to love. Then suddenly, you appeared."

    - innocent
    - sad
    - regal
    - bratty
    - amused
    - disgusted
    - thrilled
    - shocked
    - doubtful

Make an effort to really get into each character. Change your speaking tone to enhance the meaning of the words (resonance vs. breathiness, warmth vs. brightness, soft vs. loud, etc.). Analyze your soft palate placement and resonance, taking note of how each tone is made. Also, pay attention to how your phrasing changes with each character (pauses, emphasized words, general speed). You will want to draw from these interpretive tools when researching, and then delivering, a lyric.

🔊 **"You Appeared" – spoken with varying character styles**
TRACK 108

6. Tonal practice, singing: Let's add a melody to our sample line. Sing the melody given below (or make up your own) repeatedly, each time employing one of the following approaches we practiced while speaking:

- innocent
- sad
- regal
- bratty
- amused
- disgusted
- thrilled
- shocked
- doubtful

🔊 **"You Appeared" – sung with varying character styles**
TRACK 109

If you feel a bit silly doing this, that's okay! That's why we do these in the privacy of our homes and not at restaurants with friends. It's important to explore tonal range and resonance options. While we always want to sound natural and sincere, tonal variety can really enhance a lyric. Storytelling is acting, and variance of tone keeps it interesting. We need to explore the boundaries of our voices to know how to use them.

For more practice on tone and character exploration, read dramatic stories aloud. Children's books work well for this type of exercise. Record yourself!

EXERCISE 3
GETTING A HANDLE ON REGISTER SHIFTS

When we have vocal understanding, control, strength, and consistency, we are able to sing anything we want to sing without fear or hesitation. Great technique also allows us the ability to change our tone and style to fit the story and musical genre. Let's explore several concepts and exercises that will be helpful on your vocal technique journey.

WHAT IS A REGISTER SHIFT?

A vocal register shift (a.k.a the vocal break, passaggio, or bridge) happens when a vocalist sings through a transition area of the voice. In these transition areas, the singer might notice a change in the feeling and/or tone of the voice – some more than others. Take note of these examples of transition areas for general voice types from the perspective of contemporary commercial singing.

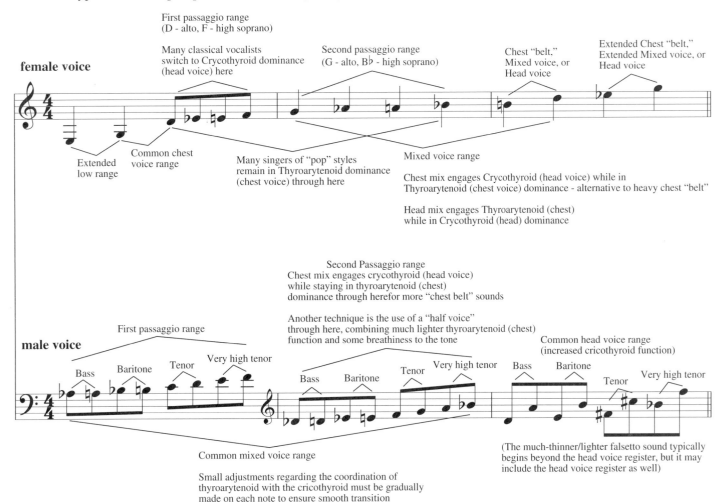

When we experience difficulty moving through these transition areas smoothly, it can have a negative effect on our sense of vocal freedom, creativity, tone, agility, and confidence. If this resonates with you, fear not! This difficulty is not unique to you, and it can be eliminated. Learning to sing with an even tone from bottom to top with smooth transition areas requires a particular type of skill and understanding. With practice, anyone can learn to do it.

We'll start with the basics: chest register and head register. Our chest register (chest voice) is our speech register. Most of us speak in chest voice. Head register (or falsetto) is the lighter upper register we find when we hoot like an owl. (There are discrepancies in how the term "head voice" is used. In this book, we will refer to "head register/falsetto" as the place where chest voice is deactivated.)

Men speak and sing primarily in their chest register. Trained male singers are typically able to blend (mix) some head register with their chest voice toward the top of their range; however, plenty of male singers, particularly basses and baritones, simply utilize their lower range without developing much head register blending. Tenors often need to develop head register blending skills as a way to expand their vocal range, because they don't have as many note options on the bottom.

Women typically speak in chest register and sing in chest voice, head voice, or a blending of the two. Women who sing exclusively in their head register, without engaging chest voice, may find it difficult to sing songs in contemporary commercial genres, because those songs tend to sit in speech range. Without the use of chest voice, it can be difficult to generate enough volume or resonance in the lower range of the voice (near middle C and below), and the tone will likely not sound authentic to the style.

In contrast, female vocalists who sing exclusively in chest voice, with no head register engagement, will experience significant tension as they ascend until they hit a "ceiling," resulting in a yodel as the voice suddenly switches into head register as a way to ease the chest voice tension.

Male vocalists who sing exclusively in chest voice, with no head register blending, will experience a "ceiling" as well if they ascend high enough in chest voice.

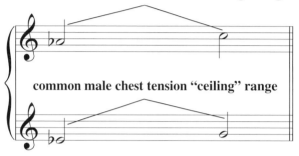

So how do we get a handle on register shifts? To do this, we need to learn how to blend (mix) head and chest registers. In my professional singing life, I sing in a lot of different styles; this requires different types of vocal technique, including several approaches to shifting registers. My students are often crossing genres and using their voices in a variety of ways as well. For this reason, I want my students to have a deep understanding of how the voice works and how they can utilize various approaches to register shifts to fit a particular genre. The following outlines the approach I typically take.

Identify Your Chest and Head Register

To locate chest register, say something loudly in a stern voice, as though someone just stole your wallet and you are shouting to them as they run away: "Hey! Hey you! Get back here!"

To locate head register/falsetto, try to imitate Elmo or Mickey Mouse, or try to hoot like an owl. Start at the top of your range and do a downward slide on "hoo."

🔊 identifying head register and chest register
TRACK 110

Test Each Register Individually

At the start of this process, it's good to get an assessment of the boundaries of the voice. Start at the bottom of your range in your chest voice where you speak. (Women, make sure you are in speech register. Say, "hey" or a loud "uh uh uh" in your speaking voice to be sure.) Ascend as high as you can without "flipping" into head voice or falsetto. If you can ascend to the top of your range without any sort of yodel or flip, then you likely already have some skill blending the two registers (or, women, you started in head voice and didn't realize it).

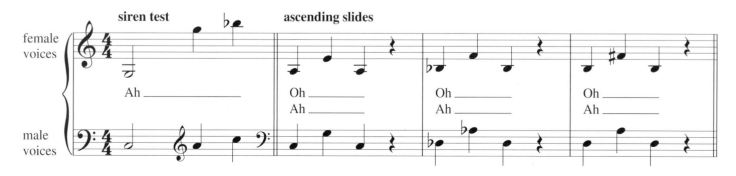

Now start at the top of your range in head register. Hoot like an owl to make sure you are in head register/falsetto. (In head register, you should feel it resonating higher in your head, less in your throat.) Try the following exercise in head register.

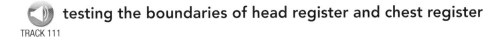

testing the boundaries of head register and chest register

TRACK 111

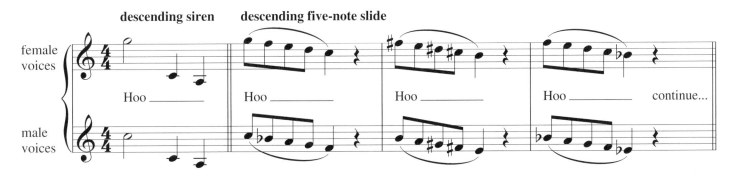

Women: It is important to note that many classically trained female singers are accustomed to bringing head voice down into their speech register, while experienced pop singers are typically accustomed to bringing chest voice high into their head register area.

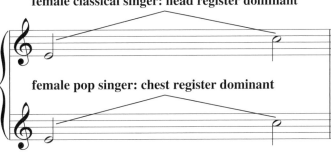

Understand the Basic Muscle Function of the Voice

Put simply, there is a chest voice muscle (thyroarytenoid muscle or TA) and a head voice muscle (cricothyroid or CT). The job of the TA is to keep the vocal cords short and thick, resulting in a chest voice placement and sound. The job of the CT muscle is to lengthen and thin the vocal cords, resulting in head voice placement. These two muscles are the big players in the larynx (voice box; see page 93), and as vocalists, we use them in tandem to blend the registers together and smooth out transition areas. When transition areas are not smooth, shifting suddenly from one register to another, this is because one muscle (TA or CT) was dominant for too long without gradually engaging the other muscle in preparation for the shift. Think of it as a see-saw that will move in super-slow motion on its way from one side to the other. If the muscles work together, making slight adjustments toward each other on every note, the result is a blending of chest and head register, also called mixed voice. The ratio of chest register to head register in mixed voice can vary, based on the dominance of the TA or CT muscle at any given time. More TA dominance will result in a chest-dominant sound. More CT involvement will result in a head-dominant sound. The goal is to have both muscles engaged during the singing process, to ensure smooth transitions from top to bottom and from bottom to top.

Want to know more about the science behind singing? Explore books and online resources devoted to the topic. For suggestions, check the resources page at the end of this book.

Become Familiar with Vocal Cord Compression

Having control over vocal cord compression is very helpful, not only for stylistic vocal delivery, but also during the mixing process. If you are in head register and want to engage the TA muscle for more chest voice in the mix, add a bit more vocal cord compression. If you are in chest voice and want to engage the CT muscle to add more head voice to the mix, decrease the vocal cord compression.

Make use of this spoken vocal cord compression exercise.

 compression awareness
TRACK 112

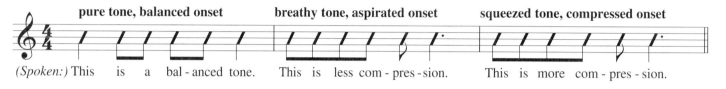

Practice Vocal Onset Variety

Along the same lines as vocal compression, vocal onset refers to the start of the note when we sing. There are three types of vocal onset: soft (aspirated or breathy), hard (glottal or exploding), and balanced. Let's practice each one with this exercise. In the second line, try alternating the onset with each note.

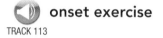 **onset exercise**
TRACK 113

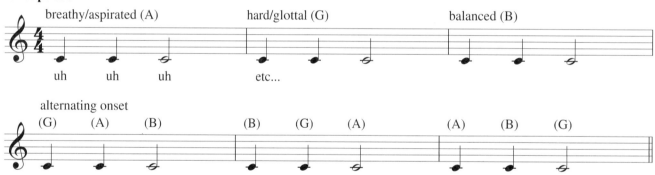

As storytellers, it is helpful for us to be able to control our vocal onset. Jazz singers like Nancy Wilson frequently use a hard/glottal vocal onset as a way to emphasize words or increase the intensity of a syncopated rhythm. Check out her rendition of "Let's Live Again." You can hear a great deal of glottal onset throughout the recording.

Practice Mixing from the Top Down

Start in head register with a glottal start, as though you just said "okay" loudly. The glottal start helps engage the TA muscle (chest voice) in a register where the CT muscle (head voice) is dominant. Slide down an octave, shifting the dominance as you go, and ending in a chest voice dominant sound. Try this on many vowels and see which one works best for you at this point. If you find the placement still too head dominant on the bottom, try increasing the vocal cord compression.

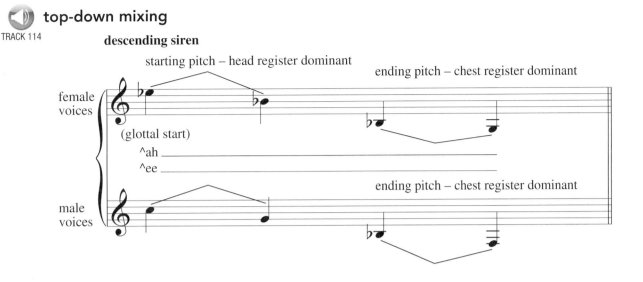

top-down mixing

descending siren

Practice Mixing from the Bottom Up

Singers who sing primarily in chest voice may find it difficult to engage the head voice muscle as they ascend. To develop chest-mix coordination, start in chest register with a balanced onset; avoid hard or glottal onsets. Slur up a major third and back down. Slur slowly at a medium-soft volume. Start a half step higher each time, taking care not to "squeeze" the vocal folds or lift the chin as you ascend. Make sure there is some lift to the soft palate, aiming for a feeling of resonance in the head as opposed to the throat. Allow the feeling of resonance to travel, moving upward as the notes ascend. Continue ascending by half step until you feel you have smoothly transitioned out of chest register dominance and into head register dominance. When you feel like you are able to blend registers, change the exercise to ascending slurs of a fifth. If this is challenging, and you experience voice cracks or simply hitting a ceiling, don't get discouraged. This is a subtle skill that can take quite a bit of time to develop.

Here are a few troubleshooting tips:

1. Check that your ears are in line with your shoulders and hips

2. Be sure to keep the chin level. It should not jut out or up at any time.

3. Try starting with a soft onset, slightly breathy at the start. Keeping a bit of breathiness to the tone means decreasing vocal fold compression. This encourages the CT muscle (head voice) to engage, even though the TA muscle (chest voice) is dominant.

4. Regardless of the vowel, try to keep your throat open (as though you are saying "oh" or "uh") as you slur up and down. This will help keep the larynx (voice box) in a neutral position instead of allowing it to ride up in your throat.

5. Try a variety of syllables as you slur (moh, ah, hmmm, ng, ney…). Some will be easier than others.

6. Make sure you aren't singing too loudly during this exercise.

7. Try humming the slurs while trying to push air out of your nose. This can usually help move resonance into the head and ease vocal fold compression.

8. Make sure you are allowing the resonance to travel up and down as the note ascends and descends.

 **bottom-up mixing**

TRACK 115

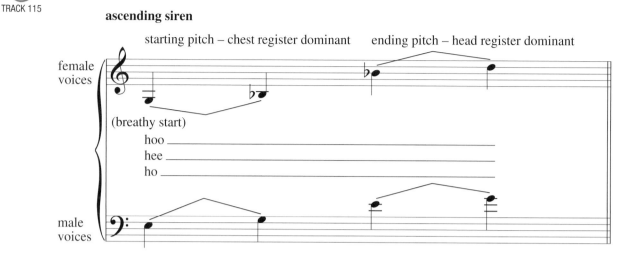

Sliding to Success

Slides are a great practice method for learning to mix head and chest registers. Remember that the resonance (where the sound feels like it is "buzzing") should be in a constant state of motion. As you ascend, allow the sound to feel like it is traveling up. Take note of the feeling and location of resonance as you slide up and down, experimenting with compression to find the right setting for each note. Try changing the ratio of CT vs. TA while doing the slides, sometimes increasing TA function, other times letting CT lead the way. It's all about exploration. Do these exercises every day. (Don't skip any days. Even just five minutes every day is more effective than an hour once a week.) Your head voice and chest voice muscles need repetition to build strength, and your brain needs repetition to build good vocal habits. By working the two registers each day, isolated and mixed together, we are seeking to avoid an imbalance in vocal muscle development.

sliding exercises

TRACK 116

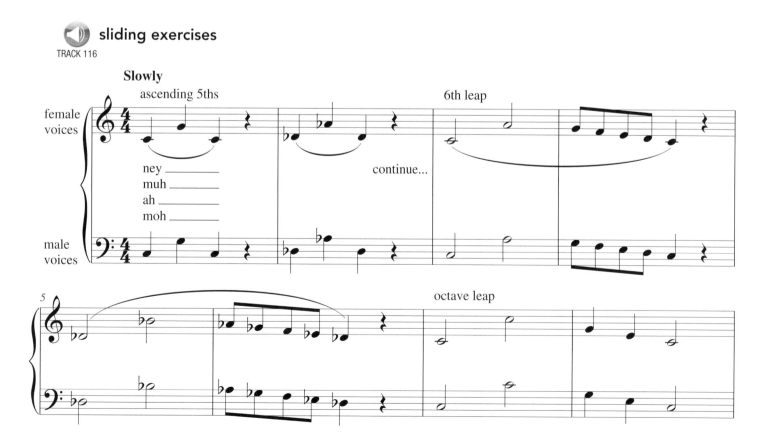

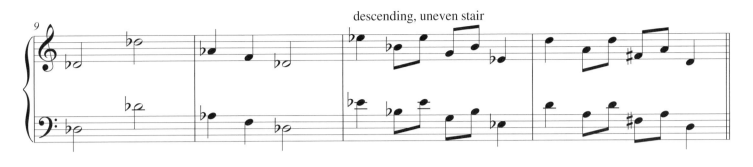

descending, uneven stair

EXERCISE 4
VIBRATO

In contemporary commercial styles of singing like pop, jazz, country, and R&B, vibrato is used as a stylistic tool rather than a constant. It is employed in a number of ways that vary greatly from genre to genre. For example, you hear a lot more vibrato from Gospel artists like CeCe Winans and Andraé Crouch than from pop artists such as Taylor Swift and Adam Levine. If you want to explore singing in different genres, take time to analyze the vibrato patterns of many singers in each style. With each vocalist you study, take note of the following:

1. What is the general speed of the vibrato? How many undulations (waves) are there per second?

2. What is the overall width of the vibrato? How far does it go above or below the original note?

3. How much is vibrato used? What percentage of notes have vibrato?

4. When vibrato is used, when does it appear in the note? Right at the start? Halfway? Only at the very end?

5. What happens dynamically during the vibrato? Does volume/intensity increase? Decrease? Stay the same?

6. Are vowels typically held open during vibrato use, or does vibrato usually happen on sustained consonants?

vibrato analysis checklist

TRACK 117

Natural Vibrato

Vibrato occurs naturally in the voice. It is usually an indicator that the vocal technique is balanced and efficient and that the outer larynx muscles are relaxed. If you cannot produce vibrato in your voice, or if it is beyond your control, it is likely a symptom of a problem in the technique somewhere else. Go back to basics: posture, breath management, soft palate lift, open throat. (Refer to the previous exercise.) The most common causes of a voice without vibrato capabilities are:

- Pushing too much air out when singing, diluting the tone (extreme breathiness)
- Too much air speed, without breathiness ("laser beam" tension)
- Flat soft palate, resulting in "throaty" singing or low resonance placement
- Little or no engagement of abdominal muscles in breath management, resulting in throat support

common causes of vibrato problems

TRACK 118

When you can achieve a natural vibrato and want to explore some vibrato options, try the following exercises.

Vibrato Width Exercise

This exercise is all about the flexibility and control of the larynx. Don't let the air speed get too fast. Use the minimum amount of "air out" you need to sing in a supported way, as opposed to pushing out more than you need. Keep things relaxed, and allow your larynx to be as loose as possible, avoiding "muscle holding." Keep your resonance high, imagining it is "buzzing" behind your nose (not in your nose, behind). Focus your ear on the top note as you allow the larynx to reach down (without micro-managing it or lowering the placement) and tap the lower note. Keeping the resonance high for both notes is the key to achieving agility here. A throaty placement is a tight placement.

vibrato width exercise

TRACK 119

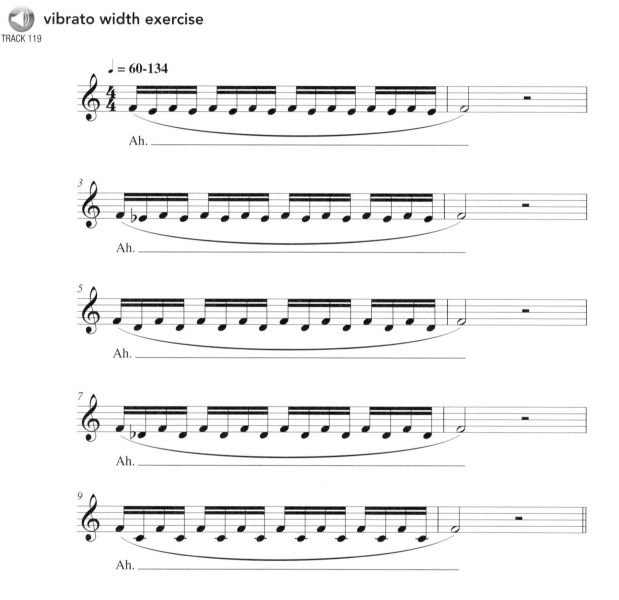

Vibrato Speed Exercise

We will now focus on the speed of the vibrato. Work to master this exercise at 100 bpm, 125 bpm, and 140 bpm. Aim for a consistent tone, consistent placement, consistent dynamic, and rhythmically controlled delivery. Slower air speed helps relax the vibrato, and increased air speed and air pressure (pushing a bit more air out faster) tends to increase the speed of vibrato. Take care not to push so much air out that you dilute the tone. In this exercise, you don't want the tone to suddenly become airy as the vibrato speed changes.

vibrato speed exercise

♩ = 100-140

smooth slur, slow air speed

Ah.

slightly more air speed and support

Vibrato Start Exercise

Set your metronome to 120 bpm. Using the vowel "ah" at a comfortable place in your range, begin singing with a straight tone, adding vibrato on beat 3. Do this exercise eight times; with each repetition, begin the vibrato a beat later than the previous time. Practice with different vowels (eh, ee, oh, oo), and sing in different areas of your range. You may also try this while singing actual words (time, play, tree, cold, soon).

vibrato start exercise

♩ = 120

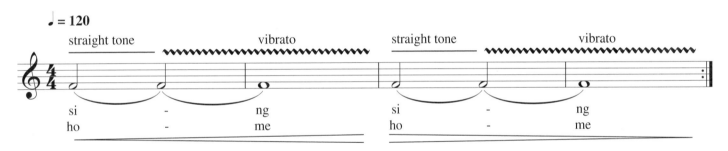

straight tone vibrato straight tone vibrato

si - ng si - ng
ho - me ho - me

Vibrato Intensity Exercise

This exercise focuses on the intensity of the vibrato at the end of a word. We've notated "sing" and "home," but any word ending in an "n" or "m" will be adequate for our purpose. Sing the etude on various pitches throughout your range. Keep your metronome at 120 bpm.

We will first practice vibrato intensity. Start singing the word softly with straight tone. After two beats, add vibrato as you crescendo (get louder) on the open vowel. Close the consonant. Continue to crescendo with vibrato on the closed consonant.

Now, we'll try the opposite effect, decreasing the vibrato intensity. Begin singing the word loudly with straight tone. After two beats, add vibrato as you diminuendo (get softer). Close the consonant. Continue to diminuendo with vibrato as you sustain the closed consonant. Allow the resonance to travel up. The soft volume will likely activate head register; depending on the note, your placement might travel into complete head register.

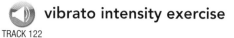
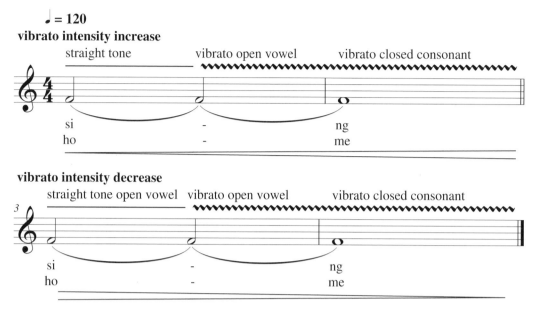

♩ = 120

vibrato intensity increase

straight tone | vibrato open vowel | vibrato closed consonant

si - ng
ho - me

vibrato intensity decrease

straight tone open vowel | vibrato open vowel | vibrato closed consonant

si - ng
ho - me

EXERCISE 5
CHOOSING A KEY WITH THE LYRIC IN MIND

For choosing the key of a song in a contemporary commercial style (like pop, jazz, folk, or rock), let's use an exercise I first heard about from my colleague at the University of North Texas, Jennifer Barnes.

First, speak a few words softly, like you are speaking to someone right next to you. Make it simple, like "Hi. How are you? Nice to see you." Repeat the phrase(s) a few times at that dynamic. See if you can sustain one of the lower pitches, then check that note on the piano. Take note of the pitch.

Second, speak a few words as though you were talking to someone across the room, louder than before, with a bit more intensity. Use phrases like "Hey, when did you get here? Great to see you." Repeat them several times. Get an idea of where that sentence sits in your voice, and see if you can identify the general pitch range on the piano.

Lastly, speak some words with great intensity. Think about calling out to your favorite player on the baseball field, shouting to your neighbor across the street, or reacting to a surprise party thrown for you. You are trying to find the higher and louder intensities in your speaking voice. Keep this in your actual speaking voice, rather than going to a character voice. (We're not looking for Mickey Mouse or Elmo sounds, for example.) Find the general range of these pitches by sustaining your speaking and checking them on the piano.

This range of pitches is the general range of your speaking voice. Use this as a guide when looking for the key of a song you want to sing. Contemporary commercial styles like pop, folk, and jazz are sung on microphone. For that reason, the keys are typically placed in speech range. There is no need to place them higher than speech range, because there is no need to project to the back of the theater or over a symphony orchestra without amplification like a classical singer would need to do.

finding your key

TRACK 123

90

CHAPTER 6
Further Tonal Exploration

EXERCISE 1
DYNAMIC VARIETY

When a vocalist sings with dynamic variety, it provides nice surprises for the audience, particularly if the chosen dynamics enhance the lyric interpretation. Dynamics can change from section to section, phrase to phrase, or even within a phrase. Check out Carmen McRae's version of "Satin Doll" from her album *The Great American Songbook.* So much dynamic variety! It makes her rendition so fun to listen to, and the lyric is always out front.

When you sing with a soft dynamic, increase your articulation energy a bit, using more exaggerated lip and tongue movements. You might also find it helpful to increase air speed, to keep the sound from becoming timid. There is a fine line between an intimate/quiet delivery and a timid/unstable delivery, so look for ways to sound intentional at soft volumes.

When you sing with louder dynamics, look to the master vocalists in that particular genre for the appropriate amount of articulation energy. My specialty is jazz, and in a traditional jazz lyric delivery, I don't need a lot of face and articulation energy when singing at a loud volume. If I use the articulators too much at a loud volume, my sound could travel out of the jazz idiom and into a more theatrical style.

Use this exercise to experiment with dynamics. Notice how the different dynamic plans each have a different effect on the meaning of the line.

🔊 **dynamics exercise**
TRACK 124

91

EXERCISE 2
RESONANCE

Resonance is a "buzzy," ringing quality to the voice that is achieved when the vocalist rings the tone in just the right spot. A resonant tone seems louder, brighter, and more pleasing to the ear than a tone that lacks resonance. Achieving a resonant tone is the primary way to sing more efficiently. Resonance allows a singer to reach louder volumes more easily, without having to squeeze the vocal cords together or overuse laryngeal muscles.

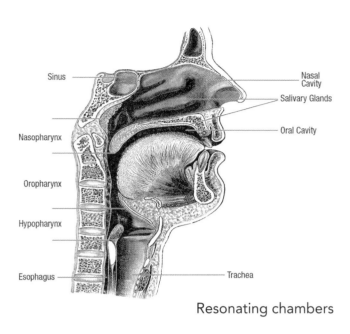

Resonating chambers

Think of it this way: Once the sound is created by the vocal cords, it journeys up three floors of the resonance track. The first floor is inside the trachea in the neck (laryngopharynx). The second floor is in and behind the mouth (oral cavity and oropharynx). The third floor is in and behind the nose (nasal cavity, nasopharynx).

Some singers try to create resonance by squeezing the vocal cords together, singing with a feeling of compression in the first floor. This is not a safe way to sing. Good vocal resonance is achieved by allowing the sound to ring in both the second and third floors. Everyone's resonating tract is different – no two heads are the same! Experimentation is the best way to find the sensations associated with healthy resonant vocal placement. We can't see our instrument as it is resonating, so we have to go by the feeling and the tone. Record yourself!

Practice the following resonance exercises and work on finding your buzzy tone. Keep in mind, these are simply tools to find the buzzy places in your face. Your tone will not sound "pretty" during this type of experimentation. Except for the final exercise below, pretty is not the goal at this stage. Buzzy is the goal. Once you find the buzzy places, you will then know where to aim the sound as you work to sing with the tone you like.

🔊 **resonance exercises**

TRACK 125

Exercise 1

Aim for buzziest, most reedy sound; it won't be pretty.
Aim behind the nose, not in it.
Experiment as you sustain to find the right place.

Ree. —————————————

Exercise 2

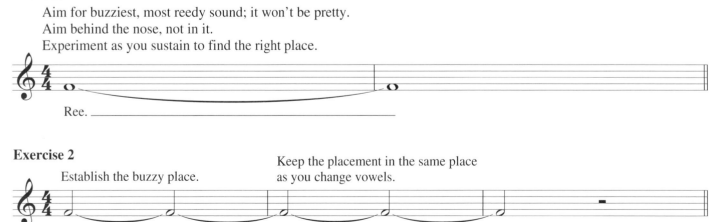

Establish the buzzy place.

Keep the placement in the same place as you change vowels.

Ree   reh   rah   roh   roo.

Exercise 3

Ring ring ring ring ring ring ring ring ri - ng, ring ring ring ring ring ring ring ring ri - ng.

Exercise 4

Ning ning ning ning ni - ng, ning ning ning ning ni - ng.
Ney ney ney ney ney, _____ ney ney ney ney ney. _____

Exercise 5

Find the buzzy place.

Open the vowel, singing with a pretty tone,
keeping the resonance.

Ree eh.

EXERCISE 3
LARYNX POSITION

Your larynx (pronounced "LAIR-inks") is your voice box. You can locate it by feeling for the V-shaped protrusion or Adam's apple in the middle of your neck; it's more prominent in men. The position of the larynx can affect tone significantly; it can also have an effect on the ease of singing and the ability to blend registers. Many respected voice pedagogues agree that neutral larynx placement – usually slightly lower than where you speak – is ideal for efficient and effective singing. I have found that when I relax and make the sound of vocal fry quietly, my larynx is in a good position. Singing low notes into a party straw usually helps singers find a good neutral larynx position. A high larynx, common in untrained singers, is often restrictive and accompanied by unwanted laryngeal muscle tension. The tone sounds thin and strained, and mixing or accessing head register is made difficult. Depressing the larynx into an unnaturally low position is equally counterproductive, usually causing the laryngeal musculature to become out-of-balance.

While singing the following exercise, keep your larynx in a neutral position. Maintain an open feeling in your throat as you ascend. If you feel your larynx want to push up, focus on holding the back of the tongue down as you ascend in pitch.

🔊 **neutral larynx exercise**

TRACK 126

Slowly (♩ = 60-80)

Muh, _____ muh. _____

As an experiment, let your larynx ride up. See if you can identify that feeling. Now depress the larynx, forcing it to go down too far while singing. Then, aim for a neutral larynx again. The goal is to have control of the larynx position.

There are certain singing techniques that call for manipulation of the larynx. For example, some chest voice belting techniques or mixing with a lot of chest voice use a high larynx position. If the singer has a strong grasp of how to sing safely and efficiently with different larynx positions, this can be quite effective. Again, experimentation is key to finding what placements and settings are right for your vocal goals from moment to moment. It helps if you can work with an experienced voice teacher as you navigate this undertaking. As with most things in life, pain is cause for alarm and increased awareness. If you feel vocal pain at any time during your vocal journey, stop and change course. Singing should never hurt!

EXERCISE 4
ANALYSIS AND IMITATION TO BUILD TONAL VARIETY

Select a recording by one of your favorite artists. Choose a small section (approximately four to eight bars) to work on. In these few measures, analyze everything you can about the tone. Go through the following tonal checklist and figure out the answers through imitation.

- How much soft palate space is the artist using? (Flat? Lightly high? Nose plugged up?)
- How open is the artist's mouth? (One finger? Three fingers?)
- How active are the articulators (tongue and lips)?
- Where is the sound aiming? (Front of mouth? Nose? Back of mouth? Roof of mouth?)
- What is the general tongue position?
- What is the general larynx position? (Low? Middle? High? Traveling?)
- What is the artist's approach to dynamics (volume)?
- What is the vocal cord compression like? (Light/breathy? Balanced? Pressed/tight?)
- How resonant is the tone? (Breathy/unfocused? Laser beam?)
- How much vibrato is used by the artist?
- If vibrato is present, what is the speed, width, frequency, and intensity?

SECTION 3
Melodic Alterations:
Shape It Like You Say It

Section 1 of this book was devoted to making thoughtful and authentic rhythmic choices when interpreting a lyric. Section 3 is all about making thoughtful melodic changes to enhance the story even more.

Is it always appropriate or effective to change melody notes?

Many jazz and pop singers make melodic changes on a repeated section, once the audience has heard the basic tune once or twice. Jazz vocalists often sing the original melody notes the first time (on the *head in*) and change them the final time (on the *head out*), with instrumental or scat singing improvisation between the *head in* and *head out*. Jazz singers also perform the tune over and over, restyling it more and more with each repetition. This type of "melodic improvisation" can take the place of *scat singing* (wordless instrumental-style improvisation) at any time. Pop singers sometimes alter the tune on a second or third verse or on a repeated chorus. Even small variations can keep things fresh and keep the listener engaged.

In this section, we will use the song "It's You." If you have skipped around in this book and haven't had a chance to learn that song, take time now to learn it *straight*, exactly as it appears on the page. You will then be able to appreciate the changes we are going to make to the song in this section.

CHAPTER 7
Small Gestures

You don't need to change every note in order to have a unique point of view. A tiny gesture on a single syllable can go a long way. Work through the following exercises to see how small, understated alterations to the melody can help deepen the point of view without straying too far from home.

EXERCISE 1
EMPHASIZING WITH HIGHER NOTES

Take a look at the first long phrase of the song "It's You." Let's refer back to our concept of establishing goal words. (For more on goal words, see Chapter 1.)

Choose an important word to emphasize. Sing it a step or two higher. (To be subtle, choose only one goal word per line.) Remember that on words with more than one syllable, the higher note should go on the syllable that is stressed.

Here are several examples of emphasis with slightly higher notes. For the sake of simplicity, and to avoid a lot of ledger lines, these examples are in the key of C. (Our lead sheet was in G.)

🔊 **small gestures, emphasizing with higher notes**

TRACK 127

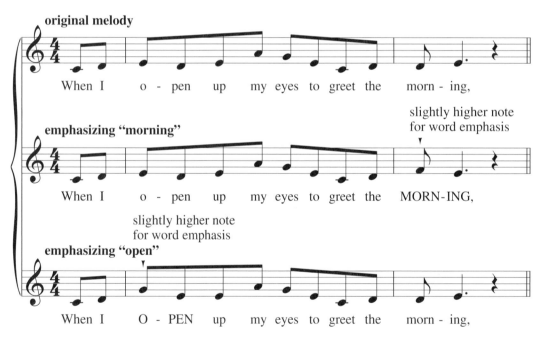

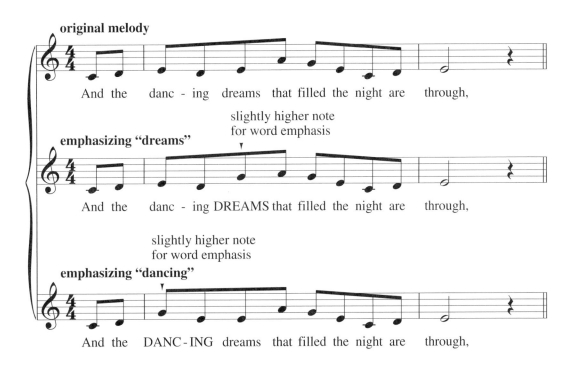

EXERCISE 2
EMPHASIZING WITH LOWER PREPARATORY NOTES

Choose a word to emphasize. In this exercise, we will leave that goal word on its original melody note, but we will find a lower pitch to sing on the word that precedes it. This can be particularly effective when we find important words on low pitches and less important words on higher pitches in the original melody. By singing less meaningful words lower, it makes the original melody notes stand out more in the interpretation.

Here are some examples of emphasizing goal words by lowering the pre-goal words.

small gestures, lower preparatory notes

TRACK 128

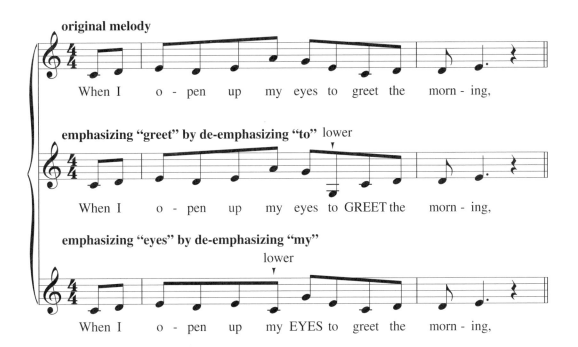

original melody

And the danc - ing dreams that filled the night are through,

emphasizing "filled" by de-emphasizing "that"

lower

And the danc - ing dreams that FILLED the night are through,

emphasizing "night" by de-emphasizing "the" lower

And the danc - ing dreams that filled the NIGHT are through,

EXERCISE 3
ADDING TONAL INTENTION

Let's color our tone a bit as we interpret this lyric. As with any good storyteller, a little variety of tone can add interest and meaning. There are many ways to enhance a lyric interpretation with tone. After analyzing many expressive vocalists and storytellers, below is a list of ideas to try as you navigate through your lyrics.

Experiment with these ideas. Sing the following lines, adding an appropriate tonal approach. Repeat them many times; with each iteration, use a different delivery concept from the corresponding emotion above.

🔊 **tonal exercises**
TRACK 129

Happy lyric moment
Bright tone, lifted face, vibrato (medium to fast speed), active articulators/facial smile.

You have made me hap - py. _____

Sad lyric moment
Neutral to warm tone, straight tone, some vibrato (slower speed), breathy tone, less active articulators/face, softer dynamic.

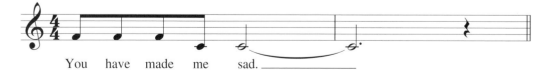

You have made me sad. _____

Surprising or magical lyric moment

Bright tone, lifted face, breathy intensity, active articulators.

Angry lyric moment

Bright tone (possibly reedy or hard), facial expression to match lyric, straight tone use, active articulators, louder dynamic, lingering consonants.

Different styles of singing call for different degrees of tonal variation. The more theatrical the style, the more tonal expression you will hear from respected singers in that genre. Focused, detailed listening to – and analysis of – esteemed vocal artists is the best way to know how far to go with changing tone color.

CHAPTER 8
Large Gestures

When a singer makes significant alterations to a melody, it can be dramatic and exciting for the listener, particularly if the changes enhance the lyric. Larger gestures can increase the overall contour of the melody, deepen the point of view, and generally keep things unpredictable for the audience, encouraging them to remain active listeners.

EXERCISE 1
TAKING GOAL WORDS EVEN HIGHER

First, let's do some harmonic homework on this tune. We want to find various note changes that fit with the chords so we can use them confidently in performance – rather than "fishing for notes" in public, which doesn't always turn out well. You can figure out new notes theoretically or by ear. Either way, it is important to practice singing these notes with an audio track. We are ear people! If it's not in our ears, it won't happen.

Using the audio track for "It's You," or playing the chords yourself, experiment with higher note options for the goal-word interpretations shown below. Take one goal word at a time, and explore at least two higher melody-note options (different from your small gesture options). These high notes may sound really out of place right now. In the next exercise, will talk about finessing them.

When I open up my EYES to greet the MORNING,
And the dancing DREAMS that FILLED the night are through,
I can hear a SWEETEST melody, a WHISPER in my ear…

 larger gestures, high-note exploration

TRACK 130

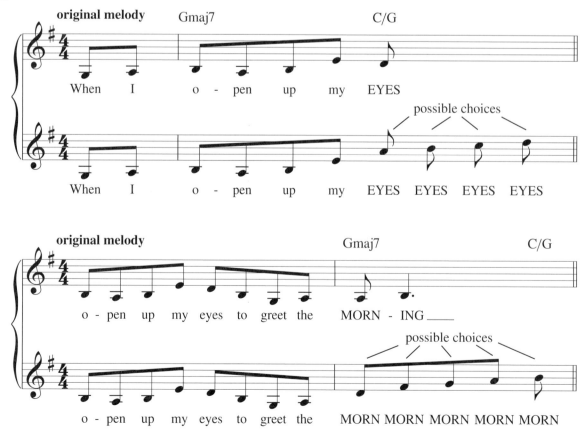

101

EXERCISE 2
FINESSING THE CHANGE

When we alter a melody note, we sometimes disrupt the original flow of the line. To avoid having our substitution sound too sudden or unnatural, we may need to finesse the variation with changes to surrounding notes. Try these options for the notes we discovered in the previous exercise.

🔊 **finessing the change**

TRACK 131

EXERCISE 3
ONE SYLLABLE, MANY NOTES
(THE SARAH VAUGHAN EFFECT)

Here, we take our cue from jazz legend Sarah Vaughan and explore adding extra notes to a target syllable. As before, let's embellish goal words while keeping meaning of the lyric. Let's look at the first line of "Dance with Me" with "extra note" concepts, written in the male key of F for simplicity of reading. Listen to Track 132 for an example of each of these concepts.

The Sarah Vaughan Effect
TRACK 132

Target Note Enclosures

Surround the target melody note with an extra note above and below. The surrounding notes can be half steps or whole steps, depending on what sounds best with the chord and to your ear.

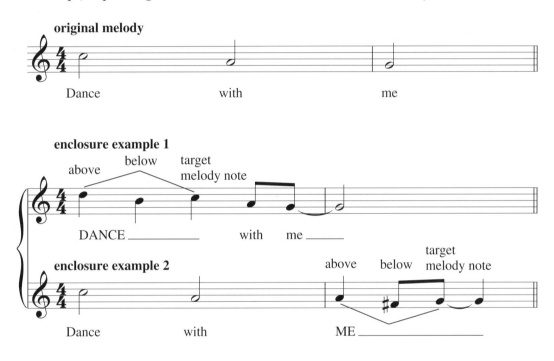

Arpeggios

An arpeggio (or "broken chord") outlines a chord. In other words, we sing the root, 3rd, and 5th of the chord. We can also extend the arpeggio to include the 7th and 9th.

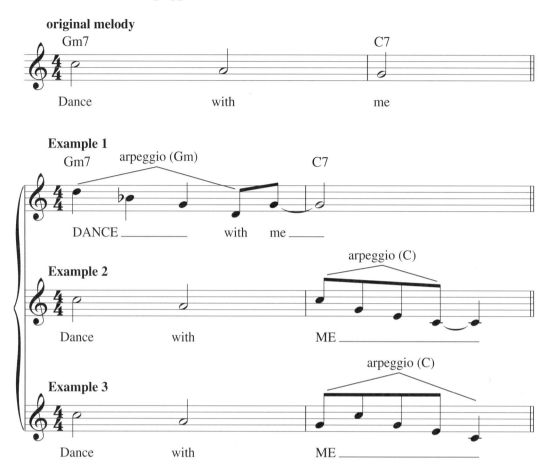

Chord Scales

Chord scales are basic diatonic scales that fit the corresponding chord. You can use parts of a scale to link words together or provide a nice shape to the line.

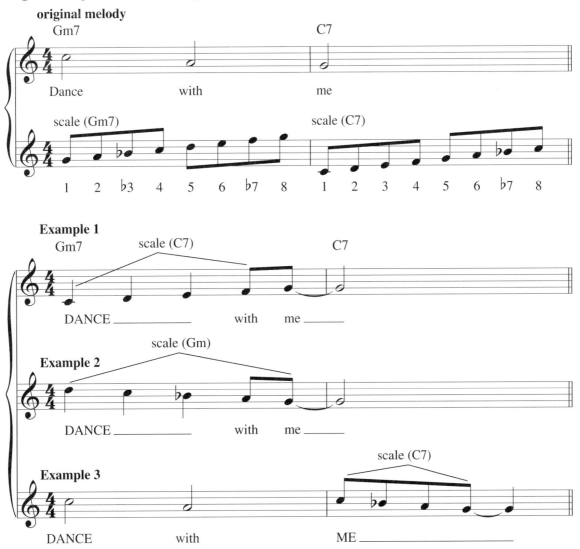

Chromatic Scales

Chromatic scales are comprised of a series of half steps. They can be an extremely effective way to add tension and release to your melody.

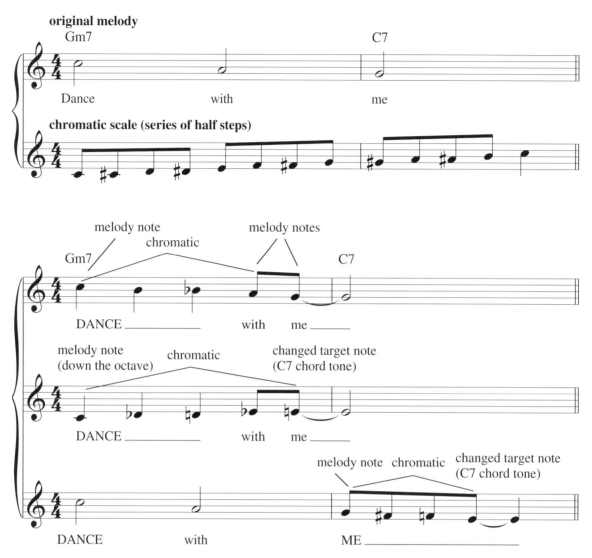

Short Sequences

Sing a short usical figure, two to four notes in length. Repeat the figure, starting on the next note of the corresponding scale, and continue the pattern as shown below. These repetitions are called sequences, and can be a useful, organized way to change the melody.

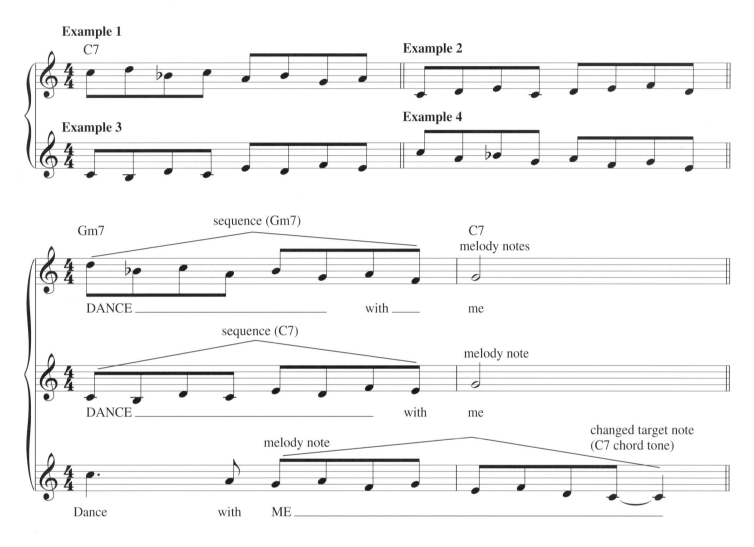

Using these tools can make changing the melody quite fun, but it can also become "unintentional" pretty quickly. To keep it intentional and stay connected to your listener, be choosy about which words you embellish with multiple notes. Goal words, usually actions and descriptive words, tend to handle this kind of treatment well. You'll find you are able to enhance the lyric as you explore your creativity.

EXERCISE 4
CONTOURING WITH OPPOSITES

Every melody has a shape, a contour. Some cover a wide range and utilize lots of leaps (e.g., "On the Sunny Side of the Street," "Cry Me a River"). Others have minimal leaps and stay in a narrower range (e.g., "Undecided," Just in Time"). We can explore changing the tune by singing it with a contour that is the opposite of the original. For example, if the original melody includes large leaps and a wide range, like "Dance with Me," it can be effective to change it my minimizing it to just one or two notes.

Minimizing Leaps

🔊 **"Dance with Me" – minimizing the melody**
TRACK 133

If the melody has a limited range, we can add leaps to expand it. Here is a line from "Ain't We Got Fun," written in 1921. The original melody does not have a lot of contour. Let's create some by adding arpeggios, along with several of the other embellishments we practiced in Exercise 3 (scales, sequences, enclosures). An octave leap is another way to enhance a melody. Sing the original melodic line, then try these three examples of expanding the contour.

🔊 **"Ain't We Got Fun" – expanding the melody**

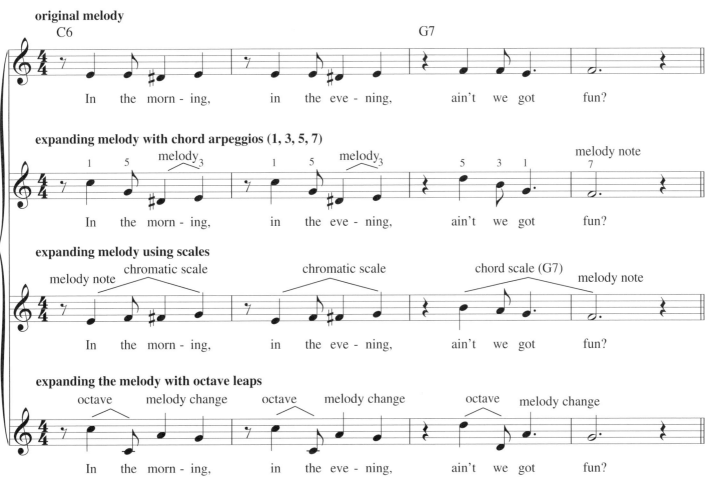

EXERCISE 5
CREATING TENSION WITH COLOR TONES

We can further enhance a lyric by adding color tones that increase the melody's harmonic tension. Each color tone has its own personality, so experiment and notice the effect each note choice has on the lyric's meaning.

The term "chord tones" refers to the root (1), 3rd, 5th, and 7th of any given chord.

The term "color tones" refers to two types of notes: extensions and alterations.

Extensions include the 9th, 11th, and 13th of a chord, extending its arpeggio above an octave.

Alterations are changes made to the 9th and 5th of a chord. Thus, the four altered-note possibilities are the ♭9th, ♯9th, ♭5th, and ♯5th. Note: You will also see ♯11 and ♭13 as alterations to a chord. While the ♯11 is the same note as the ♭5 and the ♭13 is the same note as the ♯5, the differences in notation have slightly different theoretical implications.

🔊 **chord tones vs. color tones and alterations**
TRACK 135

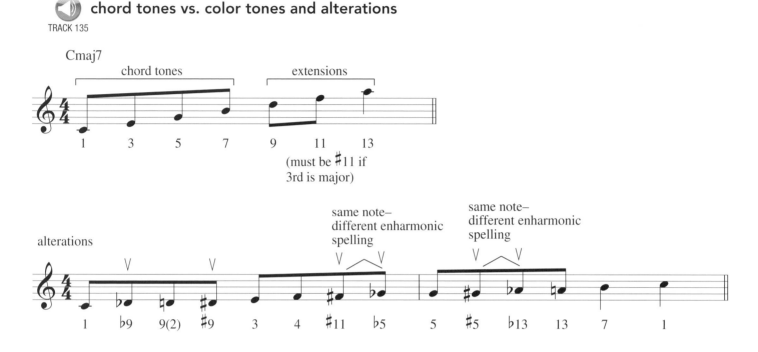

For this exercise, we'll target these three potentially "sensitive" spots in our ballad, "It's You." The goal words, in all caps, will receive the harmonic tension. Sing through the options for each spot; these include possible ways to finesse the changes. (For more on finessing the change, refer to Exercise 2 in this chapter.)

"With a sudden RAIN" (bar 24)

"I wonder how I'll EVER make it through" (bar 27)

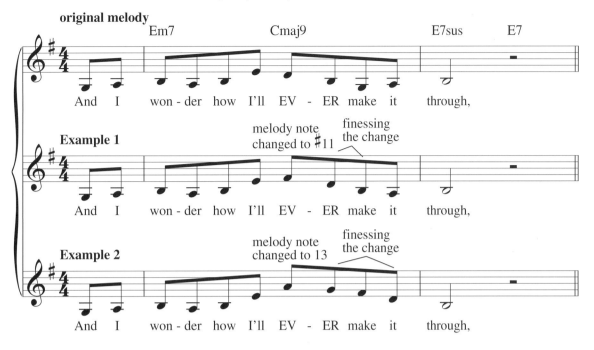

The repeated words "It's You"

The words "It's You" happens over different chords throughout the piece. Here are two versions to try:

Second "It's You" in bar 8 (incomplete cadence)

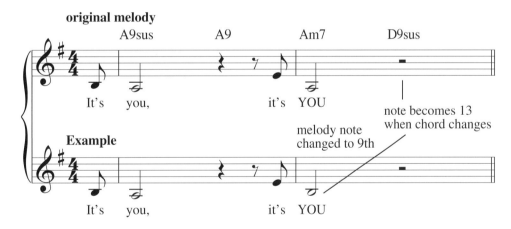

First "It's You" in bar 15 or bar 33

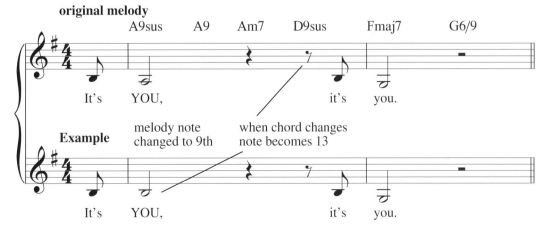

🔊 **changing melody with color tones and alterations**

If you want to dig further into the theory behind adding color tones and alterations to chords, there's a chord guide sheet on pages 130-131. The guide sheet shows the color tones and alterations that typically are added to specific types of chords.

EXERCISE 6
MATCHING RANGE WITH EMOTION

When changing the melody, it can be effective to let the emotion of the lyric determine the range of singing from phrase to phrase. Quiet emotions (sadness, intimate or shy romance, loneliness) can be sung in a lower range to deepen those sentiments. In contrast, louder emotions (joy, anger, humor) can be sung in a higher range to exaggerate those feelings.

Here is an example of taking the emotion, and thus, the range, higher for an entire phrase. This phrase was chosen because it is a possible climactic and loud moment in the song.

🔊 **changing the melody, high emotional range**

TRACK 137

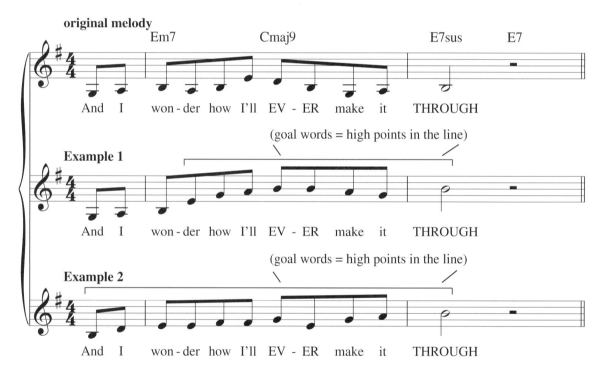

In contrast, here is an example of a possible soft, intimate moment. In the examples that follow, our intent is to extend the feeling of intimacy by singing the entire phrase in a lower range. The final two words, "yesterday's embrace," could be considered the most delicate moment in the phrase. Eliminating the leaps in the melody at that point can create a feeling of simplicity, closeness, or even melancholy. The facial expression and dynamic that accompany this moment of melodic alteration will help establish the point of view.

changing the melody, low emotional range

TRACK 138

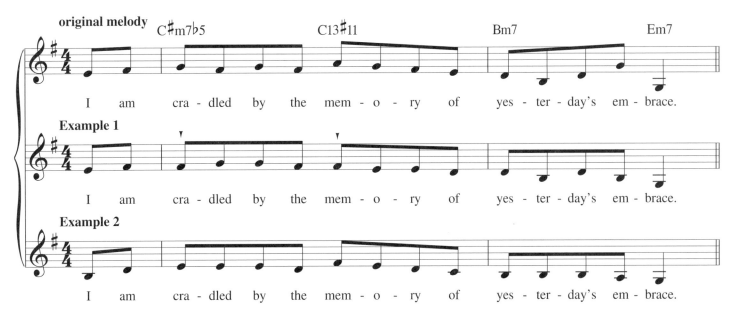

EXERCISE 7
BRINGING IN THE BLUES

Let's add the sound of the blues into our melody by using elements of the minor blues scale. This scale works well with melodies, or portions thereof, that are in a minor key.

It is especially appropriate to use this scale if you are singing a song about the blues or one with blues chord changes – like "Alright, Okay, You Win," "Stormy Monday," "Centerpiece," or "Route 66." The first four notes are most commonly used when adding this sound to your melody, but you should experiment with the entire scale. It can enhance a mournful lyric or those with attitude, anger, sarcasm, or sass. As an example, we'll use our swing song, "Dance with Me," adding a bit of minor blues to the last line.

"Dance with Me" – adding minor blues scale

TRACK 139

BONUS!
SPONTANEITY PRACTICE

Take an excerpt from a poem, newspaper article, or novel and sing the text with an improvised melody. Choose a rhythmic approach that matches the tone of the excerpt, and make up a melody that coincides with the meaning of the lyric. Remember that using higher range can emphasize words and using low range can de-emphasize words. Match the ends of your melodic phrases with the ends of sentences.

Listen to Track 135 to hear me improvise a melody to the text in this paragraph!

spontaneity practice – improvising a melody

TRACK 140

SECTION 4
Style:
Express It Like You Say It

CHAPTER 9
Exploring Stylistic Gestures

All of my favorite singers have a unique style, using particular vocal delivery techniques to create "ear candy" as they tell their story. As with everything we have explored in this book, use these techniques thoughtfully and with purpose. That way, you can express both a style and a point of view.

EXERCISE 1
SCOOPS

Scoops are used frequently in jazz and pop styles. When singers scoop into a note, they land slightly below the target pitch and slide up. The lower starting note is typically a half step or so beneath the final landing pitch.

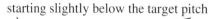

Some artists start as much as a whole step lower than the goal pitch. (For example, check out the opening line to Patsy Cline's "I Fall to Pieces.") Some singers might not start a full half step below the goal pitch. Some scoop very quickly, while others take a bit more time, particularly on a slower song. Pay attention to this kind of detail when listening to your favorite vocalists. That way, you can get an idea of their scoop style. Imitation is the best way to get a handle on these types of technique.

Scoops are used in three ways:
- Scooping the first note of a phrase as a way to begin in a gentler or more stylish way.
- Scooping a high note as a way to "soften" the approach, particularly after a leap.
- Scooping goal words as a way to add emphasis.

Try these two scoop patterns on "Dance with Me."

🔊 **"Dance with Me" – scoops**
TRACK 141

A variation on the scoop is the "down scoop," a reverse scoop that approaches the target pitch from above, usually by a half step. This type of scoop is often used in styles such as pop, R&B, and country.

starting slightly above the target pitch

Below are two melodic variations on the last line of "Dance with Me," using a down scoop. This technique feels particularly natural after a leap down, as in both examples. It can also work well accompanying sounds of the minor blues scale. For example, below we are leaping down to the "2" of the chord, which puts the starting note of the down scoop on the "blue" note, the ♭3rd of the minor blues scale.

"Dance with Me" – down scoops

TRACK 142

EXERCISE 2
SLIDES

Sliding slowly from one note to the next can have a dramatic effect. If sung with a light or breathy voice, it can create a feeling of whimsy, relaxation, or sadness. If done with a focused tone, the result can be more aggressive, adding drama to the moment. The distance between the two notes and the relative focus of tone determine the overall emotional effect. Dramatic slides don't sound at home in every style, so again, listening, analysis, and imitation are the best ways to be sure you are using these techniques tastefully and appropriately for the style: In jazz singing, it is common to hear small slides (whole step apart), whereas in pop music, big dramatic slides over large intervals are more regularly heard.

slides

TRACK 143

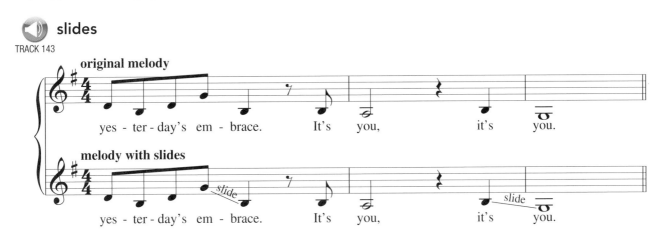

EXERCISE 3
GLOTTAL ATTACKS

In Chapter 5, Exercise 4, we discussed the various types of vocal onset, including glottal (hard) onset. Glottal attacks can be done on words that start with a vowel. When starting a note with a glottal attack, we are essentially bringing our vocal cords together more aggressively, releasing into the note a bit more explosively. For the most part, you want to employ a balanced onset, not slamming your vocal cords together! However, many artists occasionally use harder, glottal attacks as a way to emphasize a lyric or add more style. If you analyze each word that starts with a vowel in the recordings of "Guess Who I Saw Today" by jazz singer Nancy Wilson and "Roar" by pop singer Katy Perry, you will hear quite a few glottal attacks.

Disclaimer: If you repeatedly sing and/or speak with hard glottal attacks, you may develop vocal fatigue (or more significant vocal injury), so be careful. There are varying degrees of glottal attack intensity, from a slightly exaggerated onset to an extreme slamming together of the cords. For this exercise, we'll aim for the feeling of a light glottal onset.

To get this feeling, say "uhm" at a medium to loud volume. You should experience a glottal attack, feeling it in your throat a bit. Most likely, the louder you speak, the more aggressive the glottal attack will be. Try singing with a few light glottal starts on this line from "Dance with Me."

"Dance with Me" – glottal attacks

TRACK 144

Could > it be > I'll fall > in love with you? ___

Glottal attacks can be used as a way to emphasize a particular rhythm (e.g., strong downbeat, syncopation) or a particularly meaningful word. Some singers use glottal attacks throughout an entire section of a song as a way to sustain a dramatic emotion.

EXERCISE 4
DESCENDING DOUBLE STEP

A descending double step is a vocal embellishment that can be done when you are moving down by whole step. Upon descending to the lower note, you quickly return to the previous note and then quickly back down to the lower note again.

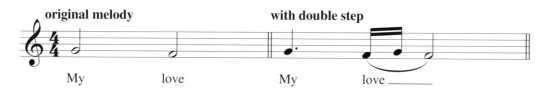

original melody — My love

with double step — My love ___

This "double step" can be done quickly in up-tempo songs with groove or a bit more slowly in a ballad style. Tip: It sounds particularly natural and smooth when the lower note begins with a vowel, an approximant (vowel-like) consonant (w, r, l), or nasal consonant (m, n). This technique can also be used as a way to add multiple notes to a single syllable.

Practice the descending double step on these excerpts from "Dance with Me" and "It's You."

descending double step

TRACK 145

EXERCISE 5
DOUBLE PULSE

A double pulse is a subtle and stylish way to emphasize goal words. It is an extra push of emphasis on an open vowel. The technique resembles scooping and re-attacking the note while sustaining the open sound, because the pitch will dip slightly between pulses.

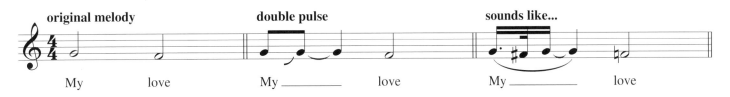

A double pulse works well with various grooves, various speeds, and in various styles. It feels particularly natural when the pulsed word is not short, but rather has a bit of time to sustain after the double pulse.

Sing double pulses on these excerpts from "Dance with Me" and "It's You."

 descending double pulse

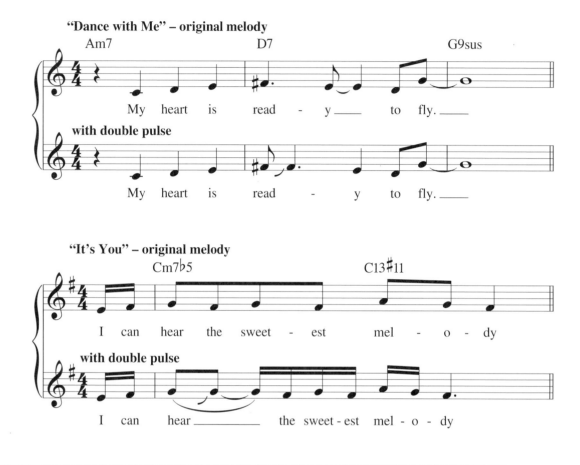

EXERCISE 6
BREATH RELEASE

You can add intensity at the end of a phrase by using an audible breath release. It feels natural to use a breath release:
- at the end of a loud and dramatic phrase.
- after an intense short note.
- after a phrase that ends rhythmically on a syncopated beat.

Breath releases are achieved by releasing the air pressure, quickly exhaling the remaining air in a quick, audible puff. The more air you have left in your lungs, the louder and more dramatic your breath release will be.

Try giving a breath release in the following exercises.

TRACK 147 **breath releases**

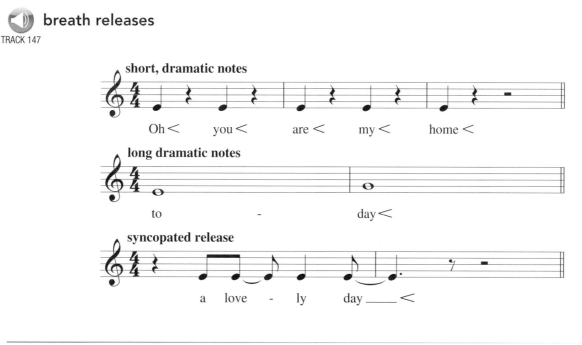

EXERCISE 7
DICTION

Many artists are known for their unique approach to diction. While it can be fun to play with pronunciation as a stylistic tool, tampering with diction also has the potential to make a singer sound insincere. It's a fine line. Some artists use diction manipulation as additional "ear candy" for the listener while others take a more natural approach, allowing the song to stand on its own. It varies from artist to artist, and you'll hear both sides of the spectrum in just about every commercial style of music.

Here are two more diction elements to study.

Vowel Height

You'll hear various approaches to vowels as you start to study your favorite artists. Some sing with a lot of space, created by either opening the mouth widely or by lifing the soft palate (or both). Others sing with a more narrowed approach. You'll find the opposite approach to that, as well as everything in between.

Example: love = luv or lahv

Diphthong Emphasis/Style

A diphthong (pronounced "DIFF-thong") occurs when there are two consecutive vowel sounds, as in words like nice, fine, I, and smile. When singing a diphthong, the emphasis is typically placed on the first vowel sound, turning to the second vowel sound toward the end of the word.

Example: mine = MAH-een

However, you might hear artists switch this concept and turn to the second vowel sound right away, sustaining that sound instead. You'll encounter this quite a bit in classic country singing.

Example: mine = mah-EEN

You might also hear the "twang" approach to diphthongs, in which the two vowels are combined into one sound. (I live in Texas, so I hear this a lot.) There are different styles of twang, but here are a couple of examples:

Examples: fire = far; smile = small

Try this line – with these three types of diction:

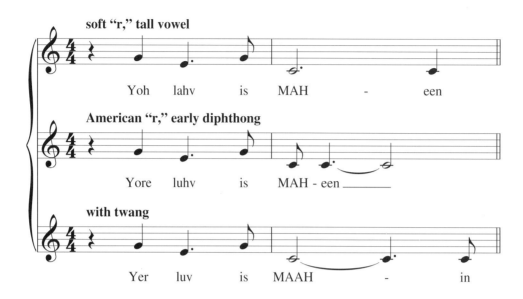

122

CHAPTER 10
Exploring Style Through Deep Transcription and Imitation

You can quickly add to your style toolbox by doing a deep transcription of another vocal artist. In this context, transcription means imitation. It isn't always necessary to write the information down, although that may help. The goal is to be able to sing along with a recording from memory, perfectly matching the style and delivery. To do this well, there are many details to analyze. Make it your goal to emulate the singer so closely that you could be hired as an impersonator of that artist. This type of deep transcription requires a layered listening approach and a lot of repetition. Here are three exercises that outline the process.

EXERCISE 1
CHOOSING A RECORDING FOR TRANSCRIPTION

Think about what you want to add to your singing style, and start a list of the various sounds/skills/artists you would like to take as a model. While it is easier to copy an artist with a singing range similar to yours, you can utilize software to raise or lower the key of the recording if you choose a song that goes outside your natural range. (There are different types of software that allow you to change the key without altering the tempo, such as Transcribe.)

Determine how much of the recording you will need to memorize to achieve your goals. For example, if you want to imitate the vibrato style of a particular singer, use a smaller section of the song – say, 4-16 measures, depending on the tempo. This way, you can do many repetitions easily, spending your mental energy on mastering the vibrato technique rather than learning a lot of lyrics and phrasing. On the other hand, if you want to memorize how a singer employs phrasing options, manipulates their tone, explores dynamics throughout a song, or embellishes the melody, you'll likely need to transcribe a longer section, or even the entire recording. This can take a great deal of time, but it is highly beneficial when done well. Deep analysis and complete memorization are key.

EXERCISE 2
TRANSCRIBING LYRIC DELIVERY

It's imitation time! Once you have chosen the song – or portion thereof – you want to transcribe, dig in. Without singing along, listen to a short section of the recording, maybe only a measure or two. Listen five to ten times (or more if needed), taking notice of as many details as you can. These details will likely include:

- Timing of the lyric
- Dynamic level(s)
- Use of vibrato and straight tone (vibrato speed, width, intensity)
- Embellishments or style (scoops, slides, etc.)
- Tonal placement (oral cavity space, resonance)
- Vocal cord compression (breathy, focused tone, etc.)
- Size of mouth opening
- Diction style

After listening several times, begin to sing along softly with the recording, closely imitating each of the elements. Once you have learned the small section, start singing at the exact volume of the recording.

Then, try it without the recording and see how you sound by yourself. Record your performance and listen back. This is the best way to truly hear the accuracy of your impersonation. Take note: The more unfamiliar the style elements in a recording, the longer it will take you to master the duplication of them. That's fine – take your time, and enjoy the process.

When you feel confident with the first two measures, go on to the next two measures. Repeat the process with those measures. Then go back and sing from the beginning of the section, all four measures. Continue to add measures one or two at a time until the entire portion is done. Again, this could take minutes, hours, days, or even longer if these are new skills for your voice. Set reasonable goals and know that it's better to do a small section with exceptional accuracy than a longer section with mistakes.

EXERCISE 3
APPLYING TRANSCRIPTION TO PERFORMANCE

Intentionality is the key to this step. Once you have developed a new style skill, find an opportunity to use it in your own repertoire. Try implementation in one of these three ways:
- Plan the exact moment in the exact song in which to try the new skill.
- Decide on the song, but improvise the moment of implementation.
- Don't plan anything, but keep the skill on the front of your mind, constantly searching for appropriate opportunities to fit it in.

Sometimes it can be fun to transcribe renditions of songs in your own repertoire. For example, if you sing "All of Me" on your gigs, you can gather a whole library of phrasing and style ideas by memorizing five different versions of the song sung by artists you admire. In that case, you could give yourself a quoting goal, like trying to quote from at least two versions during your performance.

SECTION 5
Additional Factors

CHAPTER 11
The Visual Effect

EXERCISE 1
EYE CONTACT

Audiences like to feel connected with the singer; however, many singers find it difficult to keep their eyes open as they deliver a lyric. Many people mistakenly think the singer needs to make eye contact with the audience. On the contrary, making eye contact with individual members of the audience can be distracting for the performer and can make the listener feel uncomfortable. You want to achieve the illusion of eye contact by looking at the tops of the listeners' heads or by focusing on the arms of the chairs rather than peoples' faces. Ideally, you want to get to a point where you can scan over an audience without really seeing them. This will help you block out the distractions, similar to closing your eyes, while still appearing to engage the audience visually. Avoid looking too high above their heads or too low to the floor. Keep your head at a comfortable position; while gazing at foreheads or tops of heads of the listeners, occasionally move your overall gaze from left, to center, to right. This way, you will avoid the look of staring at one safe place.

To apply this, pick three spots in your line of vision. One should be on the left side of the room, another on the right side, and another in the middle. Practice singing through one of your songs, switching your focal point every few phrases. Take it a step further and draw pictures of imaginary heads, securing them in the general area of the three focal points. Then, practice aiming your gaze at the top of their heads while alternating between the three focal points.

EXERCISE 2
FACIAL EXPRESSION AND INVOLVEMENT

The expression on a singer's face can affect many aspects of the performance, including:
- Performer's vocal tone
- Perceived interpretation of the lyric
- The listener's feeling of connection to the performer
- The listener's perception of the confidence level of the performer

Different genres have different traditions regarding how much facial involvement is idiomatic, but it's obvious that renowned singers are active with their faces in some way, no matter what the musical style.

You can improve your facial involvement by doing a "facial transcription." This means memorizing the facial expressions of another singer as they perform. The facial transcription should be done in as detailed a manner as a vocal transcription, imitating and memorizing the actual singing.

If you feel you don't typically use your face much when you sing, repeat the following line with varying degrees of facial involvement.

"I also use my face to deliver these lyrics. Can you tell?"

🔊 **facial expression degrees**
TRACK 149

- 10 percent: no eyebrow involvement, minimal mouth opening, not much facial expression
- 30 percent: slight eyebrow lifting on key words, slightly more articulation energy and mouth opening
- 60 percent: significant eyebrow lifting on key words, significant articulation and mouth energy
- 100 percent: the most height on eyebrow lifting, the most articulation energy and size of mouth

EXERCISE 3
BODY LANGUAGE

An audience can determine a lot from a singer's body language, including whether a singer is:

- Experienced, and thus generally relaxed, as a performer in front of an audience
- Comfortable with their own body and voice
- Comfortable and prepared with the song (lyrics, song range, theme)
- Comfortable with the band

Record a video of yourself singing in front of an audience. This is the best way to analyze your own body language. If you don't yet do much performing, a video recording of a practice session is the next best thing, particularly if you are trying your best to "perform" during that practice session. Here is a checklist you can use during your analysis:

1. How is your posture?

    You should have aligned posture (ears aligned with shoulders, aligned with hips, aligned with knees, etc.). Your shoulders should not be slouched, but rather, rolled back. Not only does this look confident, but it also helps with singing technique.

2. What is your "non-microphone" arm/hand doing?

    If you have a microphone in one hand, what is happening with the other hand? It should not be glued in any one position for an entire performance. The arm and hand can hang comfortably down by your side, and you can gesture occasionally when the lyric motivates. If there is a rhythmic groove to the song you are singing, it would be appropriate to reflect the groove with your hand. Lightly tapping the beat on your leg or pulsing the non-mic hand in the air are common ways to lightly reflect the groove. Watch videos of respected performers in your genre to find a good model to imitate. The amount of physical involvement with a groove varies from one musical style to another. We can get into "authenticity trouble" if we try to apply elements from one genre to another that has very different visual performance traditions.

3. What are your legs/feet doing?

    Most of the time, your legs can be shoulder-width apart or a little closer together than that. It is a good neutral position. Standing with them too close together or too far apart is not as natural, conveying more of a "character" stance. If the song has a rhythmic groove, it is fitting to reflect that in your body. It can be shown subtly by tapping a heel to the beat or shifting your weight from heel to heel; the groove can be reflected even more noticeably by walking or dancing in place. It's all about tradition. What do respected performers in this genre do with their legs and feet on this type of song?

Other body language elements to consider:
Instrumental Solo

When someone in the band is taking a solo, it's considerate to look at them as they do so. It also helps the audience know where to look during that time. It is inconsiderate to take away from the solo visually by doing elaborate dancing, unless dancing is supposed to be the focal point of that moment. Also, avoid talking to someone else during another person's solo. Don't "zone out" or get distracted; it not only looks bad, but you could lose your place in the song form and forget to begin singing again!

Lyric Error

If you make a mistake with a lyric, don't let it show visually. Most likely, the audience won't notice. If you can make up another lyric in its place or replace it with lyrics from another part of the song, those are likely the best options. If you need to start singing "nonsense words" as place holders, do it. Again, there's a good chance the audience will simply think you are mumbling.

Band Error

If someone in your band makes an error, ignore it and continue as though everything is fine. If an instrumentalist gets lost in the form, another player will probably help them recover. As the band figures things out, the singer should strive to keep the audience's attention. If you need to step in and help the band find their place in the song, do so as calmly and quickly as possible, with a smile on your face. Preserving the audience experience is important and possible.

EXERCISE 4
MICROPHONE TECHNIQUE

Hand-held microphones are typically dynamic microphones, as opposed to condenser microphones. Dynamic microphones are meant to be held close to the sound source. Condenser microphones are much more sensitive and pick up sound differently, so there can be more play with proximity.

When singing with a dynamic microphone at a medium volume, the head of the microphone should be approximately one to two inches away from the lips. For softer volumes, hold the microphone closer (a half-inch); for louder volumes, hold it farther away (three to four inches). By bringing the microphone closer to your lips, you'll enhance the low frequencies of the vocal tone. On the flipside, the farther away the microphone, the less those low frequencies are enhanced. In other words, as you pull the microphone away from your face, the sound will start to thin and lose warmth. Past about four inches, the microphone will have a more difficult time picking up the sound of the voice. Increasing the gain (volume sensitivity) of the microphone can help it pick up sounds that are farther away, but the microphone becomes more vulnerable to feedback – the unwelcome squeals or low hums you hear when there is an overload in one particular frequency.

The angle of the microphone should be about 45 degrees, coming out of your mouth.

Lastly, it looks quite natural if you hold the microphone with your fingertips rather than gripping it with your entire hand. The microphone is usually held at the halfway point between the bottom and top of the mic. Again, watch videos of respected artists in your genre to determine tradition with mic technique. For example, many rap artists wrap their hand around the head of the microphone and place their lips directly on the mic. The sonic distortion that results is part of their style. However, such an approach would likely look and sound out of place if used by a jazz singer.

CHAPTER 12
Choosing Repertoire

It is beneficial for musicians to develop a broad knowledge of classic well-known repertoire in addition to exploring new and contemporary music. When musicians know the same songs, they can easily play together. In the genre of jazz, part of the tradition involves players and singers casually getting together to jam on tunes, singing and playing songs commonly known in the jazz community (standards). As we have discussed, it is exciting to hear a musician deliver a unique interpretation of a familiar song. If you don't know the songs everyone else knows, you could miss out on a big part of the culture. Learning a lot of tunes not only gives you lots of practice interpreting different melodies and lyrics, but it also helps you discover which stories you find relatable and which are more difficult to tell.

When it comes time to program repertoire for a public performance, there are many factors involved: style, vocal range, melodic interest, chord changes, and – most important to me – lyric content. When I sing songs, it helps if they fall into one of these two categories:

- Direct relation: I am singing about what I know or have observed personally in my past.
- Imagined relation: I am putting myself in someone else's shoes, playing a role, imagining what it is like to have experienced the events and feelings in the lyric.

Many singers find it easier to interpret songs with stories they can relate to directly. Imagined relation can be a little more difficult. You have to put on your acting hat and play a part. For me, "Too Young to Go Steady" is that type of song. I'm a married woman with a child, a mortgage, and a full-time job. I'm definitely not too young to go steady. However, I can think back to what it was like. As with the theater, not every role is a good fit for a particular actor. There are some stories I have a hard time telling, even when I try my best to imagine myself in their shoes. For example, "It Was a Very Good Year," made popular by Frank Sinatra, is a story I love, but I find it difficult to tell that story myself, one told from a strongly male perspective. I don't think I would ever be "cast" for that role, so it's not likely I would ever choose to perform that song. However, I know the song.

If you are at the stage in your musical journey in which finding your artistic voice is a top priority, consider repertoire choice as a significant component to that journey. What kind of stories do you want to tell? What do you want to share with your audience? What kind of emotional, technical, interpretive, and stylistic opportunities do you want to create for yourself and your band? Through listening, artist imitation, musical experimentation, and self-analysis, you will develop the skills you need to sing your stories in a way that is authentic and adventurous. You will find your voice. Have fun!

COLOR TONE POSSIBILITIES

Chord Tones: The root, 3rd, 5th, and 7th of a chord (or the 6th can substitute for the 7th)
Extensions: The 9th, 11th, 13th of a chord
Alterations: Chromatic raising or lowering of the 5th or 9th of the chord
Note: Enharmonic spelling varies for alterations (♯5 = ♭13; ♭5 = ♯11)

Major

Major	1, 3, 5	(C)
Major 6	1, 3, 5, 6	(C6)
Major 7	1, 3, 5, 7	(Cmaj7, CΔ7)

Minor

Minor	1, ♭3, 5	(Cmin, Cmi, C-)
Minor 6	1, ♭3, 5, 6	(Cmin6, C-6)
Minor 7	1, ♭3, 5, ♭7	(Cmin7, C-7)

Note: maj7 is typically used as a color tone when there is no ♭7 present.

For example, a ♮7 can be sung in these two chords:

130

Dominant

Dominant 7   1, 3, 5, ♭7   (C7)
Dominant 9   1, 3, 5, ♭7, 9   (C9)
Dominant 13   1, 3, 5, ♭7, 9, 13   (C13)

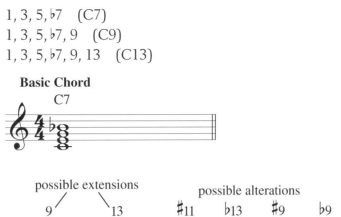

Half Diminished   ∅

Half diminished   1, ♭3, ♭5, ♭7   (Cmin7♭5 or C∅)

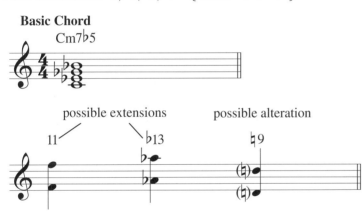

Note: The ♭9 is part of the Phrygian scale, which goes with this chord type. It can work well when sung as part of a scale or pattern. When sustained, the half step relationship to the root can be tough on the ear, particularly when sung with lyric. ♮9 is used more commonly for sustained moments with lyric.

Diminished

Fully diminished 1, ♭3, ♭5, ♭♭7   (Cdim or C°)

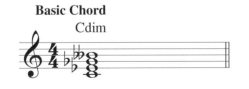

Note: These notes are all a whole step above each chord tone.

SUPPLEMENTAL LISTENING

Rubato Ballad
"Loving You" – Shirley Horn (from *Loving You*)
"God Bless the Child" – Gregory Porter (from *Be Good*)

Rubato/Straight Ballad Combination
"I Fall in Love Too Easily" – Gregory Porter (from *Liquid Spirit*)
"How Long Has This Been Going On" – Maureen McGovern (from *Naughty Baby*)
"Glad to Be Unhappy" – Nancy Wilson (from *The Great American Songbook*)
"I'm Through with Love" – Mark Murphy (from *Once to Every Heart*)
"Guess Who I Saw Today" – Nancy Wilson (from *Guess Who I Saw Today*)

Straight Ballad
"I Could Have Told You" – Shirley Horn (from *Travelin' Light*)
"February" – Jo Lawry (from *I Want to Be Happy*)

Slow Swing
"Loverman" – Rebecca Parris (from *My Foolish Heart*)
"Satin Doll" – Carmen McRae (from *The Great American Songbook*)
"I Thought About You" – Dena DeRose (from *Love's Holiday*)

Medium Swing
"Old Country" – Dianne Reeves (from *The Grand Encounter*)
"Thou Swell" – Sarah Vaughan (from *Sarah Vaughan at Mister Kelly's, Live 1957*)
"Sometimes I'm Happy" – Betty Carter and Carmen McRae
      (from *Carmen McRae and Betty Carter Duets*)
*"You Send Me" – Rachelle Ferrelle (from *First Instrument*)
"Just Squeeze Me" – Tierney Sutton (from *Blue in Green*)
      Note: First chorus performed with a New Orleans style Second Line Groove

Fast Swing
"This Can't Be Love" – Cyrille Aimée (from *Cyrille Aimée and the Surreal Band*)
"I Wanna Be Happy" – Kitty Margolis (from *Left Coast Life*)
"Hello, Haven't I Seen You Before" – Dianne Reeves (from *Quiet After the Storm*)

Bossa Nova/Medium Straight-Eighth
*"They Can't Take That Away from Me" – Eliane Elias (from *Bossa Nova Stories*)
"Soon as I Get Home" – Lizz Wright (from *Salt*)
      Note: Rubato intro
"Águas De Março" – Antonio Carlos Jobim and Elis Regina (from *Elis and Tom*)

Up-Tempo Samba
"Tim Tim Por Tim Tim" – Luciana Souza (from *Duos III*)
*"All the Things You Are" – Julia Dollison (from *Observatory*)
*"Little Suede Shoes/Day by Day" – Nancy King and Fred Hersch (from *Live at the Jazz Standard*)
"Flor De Lis" – Djavan (from *Grandes Sucessos*)

Cha-Cha
*"Days of Wine and Roses" – Poncho Sanchez (from *Soul of the Conga*) (instrumental)
"I Need to Know" ("Dimelo") – Marc Anthony (from *Marc Anthony*)
"Sway" – Michael Bublé (from *Michael Bublé*)

Mambo/Salsa
"Mi Tierra" – Gloria Estefan (from *Mi Tierra*)
* "I Won't Dance" – Nnenna Freelon (from *Maiden Voyage*)
*"Take the A Train" – Tito Rodriguez (from *Live at Birdland*)

Backbeat Styles (R&B, Funk, Hip Hop, etc.)
*"On Broadway" – Kurt Elling (from *1619 Broadway – The Brill Building Project*)
*"Our Love is Here to Stay" – Rebecca Parris (from *Gary Burton and Rebecca Parris, It's Another Day*)
*"Your Mind is On Vacation" – Marlena Shaw (from *Elemental Soul*)
*"I Got Lost in His Arms" – Terri Lyne Carrington/Gretchen Parlato (from *The Mosaic Project*)
*"I Could Have Danced All Night" – Jamie Cullum (from *Twentysomthing*)
*"Can't Take My Eyes Off of You" – Lauryn Hill (from *The Miseducation of Lauryn Hill*)

Reggae
*"My Cherie Amour" – Jazz Jamaica (from *Motorcity Roots*)
"Get Up, Stand Up" – Bob Marley (from *Burnin'*)
*"Here Comes the Sun" – Peter Tosh (from *The Best of Peter Tosh*)

7/4 (4+3)
*"Our Love is Here to Stay" – Chico Pinheiro (from *There's a Storm Inside*)
*"Tea for Two" – Sara Gazarek (from *Blossom and Bee*)
        Note: Intro is rubato, bars 9-16 are in 3/4, there are occasional bars of 4/4
*"So in Love" – Kim Nazarian (from *Some Morning*)
        Note: Bridge is in 3/4 time

5/4 (3+2)
*"Cuerpo y Alma" ("Body and Soul") – Esperanza Spalding (from *Esperanza*)
*"Bluesette" – Rhiannon (from *Bowl Full of Sound*)
"As Long as You're Living" – Cyrille Aimée (from *Cyrille Aimée and the Surreal Band*)

Double-Time-Feel Samba
*"It Might As Well Be Spring" – Stacey Kent (from *In Love Again*)
*"My Foolish Heart" – Jane Monheit (from *Never Never Land*)
*"Misty" – Richard "Groove" Holmes (from *Soul Message*)

*Denotes a particularly creative "cover" of a song. For these, I suggest listening to the original recording to appreciate the creative arrangement.

RECOMMENDED RESOURES

There are many wonderful resources available about solo singing, musicianship, and improvisation. Here is a list of some of my favorite books and websites I use for my own study and teaching.

Vocal Technique

The Structure of Singing by Richard Miller (Schirmer Books, 1986)

The Vocal Athlete by Marci Daniels Rosenberg & Wendy DeLeo LeBorgne (Plural Publishing, 2014)

Belting: A Guide to Healthy, Powerful Singing by Jeannie Gagné (Berklee Press, 2015)

Funky 'n Fun by Kim Chandler (CD series with exercises for technique/ear training/style) (www.funkynfun.com)

Singwise.com – Karyn O'Conner

New York Vocal Coaching (YouTube channel) – Justin Stoney

VoiceScienceWorks.org

Jazz Singing/Song Delivery

The Jazz Singer's Handbook by Michele Weir (Alfred Music, 2005)

Sing Your Story by Jay Clayton (Alfred Music, 2015)

Musicianship

Jazz Piano Handbook by Michele Weir (Alfred Music, 2007)

Musicianship for the Jazz Vocalist by Nancy Marano (Alfred Music, 2015)

The Jazz Language by Dan Haerle (Alfred Music, 1982)

Improvisation

Vocal River by Rhiannon (Rhiannon Music, 2013)

Vocal Improvisation by Michele Weir (Alfred Music, 2015)

Circle Songs: The Method by Roger Treece (www.rogertreece.com)

Vocal Jazz Improvisation: An Instrumental Approach by Darmon Meader (darmonmeader.com)

Jazz Conception: Voice by Jim Snidero (Advance Music, 2015)

Vocal Improvisation by Bob Stoloff (Berklee Press, 2012)

ACKNOWLEDGMENTS

Thank you to my family and friends, University of North Texas colleagues, the team at Hal Leonard LLC, and the Facebook music community; especially to Gary and Noielle Eckert, Bob and Rosemary Calderon, Jennifer Barnes, Mike Steinel, William Joyner, Sharon Burch, Peter Eldridge, Greg Jasperse, Paris Rutherford, Michele Weir, John Murphy, Olivia Gonzalez, Steve Barnes, Brian Piper, John Adams, Kent Stump, Bruce Bush, Ben Culli, and J. Mark Baker.

ABOUT THE AUTHOR

Rosana Eckert is an internationally recognized jazz vocalist, composer, and educator. She has performed throughout the U.S. and abroad with a long list of jazz luminaries, including Bobby McFerrin, Kenny Wheeler, George Duke, Christian McBride, Jon Faddis, New York Voices, and Lyle Mays. Her recordings *At the End of the Day* and *Small Hotel* have received critical recognition; *At the End of the Day* was a finalist for Best New Jazz Album in the 2006 Independent Music Awards. In addition to leading her own band, Rosana sings with the Lone Star Jazz Quintet, and co-leads Brasuka, a Brazilian-inspired original music project. Her work teaching jazz voice, songwriting, and vocal pedagogy at the University of North Texas has helped established UNT as one of the premier jazz vocal programs in the world.

A multifaceted musician, Rosana is in demand as a clinician, festival adjudicator, jazz honor choir conductor, and commissioned choral composer/arranger. Her many vocal ensemble arrangements have been performed worldwide. Passionate about sharing jazz with young students, she co-wrote, with Sharon Burch, *Freddie the Frog and the Jungle Jazz* (a musical for young voices) and *Jazz for Kids* (a song and classroom activity collection). A highly respected improviser, Rosana can be heard on *Scatability*, a vocal improvisation app by Michele Weir and on the demonstration CD for Darmon Meader's *Vocal Jazz Improvisation: An Instrumental Approach*.

In addition to her extensive live performing, writing, and teaching, Rosana works regularly as a studio vocalist, producer, and voice-over actor in Dallas. She has worked on hundreds of commercials, industrial productions, albums, publishing demos, and radio IDs heard around the world.

Originally from El Paso, TX, Rosana received a bachelor's degree in music theory and French horn performance, as well as a master's degree in jazz voice, from the University of North Texas.
www.rosanaeckert.com

ORIGINAL KEYS FOR SINGERS

Titles in the Original Keys for Singers series are designed for vocalists looking for authentic transcriptions from their favorite artists. The books transcribe famous vocal performances exactly as recorded and provide piano accompaniment parts so that you can perform or pratice exactly as Ella or Patsy or Josh!

ACROSS THE UNIVERSE
00307010..$19.95

ADELE
00155395..$19.99

LOUIS ARMSTRONG
00307029..$19.99

THE BEATLES
00307400..$19.99

BROADWAY HITS (FEMALE SINGERS)
00119085..$19.99

BROADWAY HITS (MALE SINGERS)
00119084..$19.99

PATSY CLINE
00740072..$22.99

ELLA FITZGERALD
00740252..$17.99

JOSH GROBAN
00306969..$19.99

BILLIE HOLIDAY
Transcribed from Historic Recordings
00740140..$17.99

ETTA JAMES: GREATEST HITS
00130427..$19.99

JAZZ DIVAS
00114959..$19.99

LADIES OF CHRISTMAS
00312192..$19.99

NANCY LAMOTT
00306995..$19.99

MEN OF CHRISTMAS
00312241..$19.99

THE BETTE MIDLER SONGBOOK
00307067..$19.99

THE BEST OF LIZA MINNELLI
00306928..$19.99

ONCE
00102569..$16.99

ELVIS PRESLEY
00138200..$19.99

SHOWSTOPPERS FOR FEMALE SINGERS
00119640..$19.99

BEST OF NINA SIMONE
00121576..$19.99

FRANK SINATRA – MORE OF HIS BEST
00307081..$19.99

TAYLOR SWIFT
00142702..$16.99

STEVE TYRELL – BACK TO BACHARACH
00307024..$16.99

SARAH VAUGHAN
00306558..$19.99

VOCAL POP
00312656 ....$19.99

ANDY WILLIAMS – CHRISTMAS COLLECTION
00307158..$17.99

ANDY WILLIAMS
00307160..$17.99

HAL•LEONARD®
www.halleonard.com

Prices, contents, and availability subject to change without notice.

0318